Biography Today

Profiles of People of Interest to Young Readers

Author Series

Volume 10

Cherie D. Abbey
Editor

615 Griswold Street • Detroit, Michigan 48226

Cherie D. Abbey, *Editor*
Kevin Hillstrom and Laurie Hillstrom, *Staff Writers*
Barry Puckett, *Research Associate*
Allison A. Jones, *Research Assistant*

Kevin Hayes, *Production Coordinator*

Omnigraphics, Inc.

* * *

Peter E. Ruffner, *Executive Vice President*
Matthew P. Barbour, *Senior Vice President*
Kay Gill, *Vice President — Directories*

* * *

Frederick G. Ruffner, Jr., Publisher

ISBN 0-7808-0464-3

This book is printed on acid-free paper meeting the ANSI Z39.48 Standard. The infinity symbol that appears above indicates that the paper in this book meets that standard.

Printed in the United States

Our Advisory Board stressed to us that we should not shy away from controversial or unconventional people in our profiles, and we have tried to follow their advice. The Advisory Board also mentioned that the sketches might be useful in reluctant reader and adult literacy programs, and we would value any comments librarians might have about the suitability of our magazine for those purposes.

Your Comments Are Welcome

Our goal is to be accurate and up-to-date, to give young readers information they can learn from and enjoy. Now we want to know what you think. Take a look at this issue of *Biography Today,* on approval. Write or call me with your comments. We want to provide an excellent source of biographical information for young people. Let us know how you think we're doing.

Cherie Abbey
Editor, *Biography Today*
Omnigraphics, Inc.
615 Griswold Street
Detroit, MI 48226
www.omnigraphics.com

David Almond 1951-

British Novelist for Children and Young Adults
Author of the Award-Winning Novels *Skellig* and *Kit's Wilderness*

BIRTH

David Almond was born on May 15, 1951, in Newcastle upon Tyne, a city in northern England. He is the son of James Arthur and Catherine (Barber) Almond.

YOUTH

Reading and writing became an important part of Almond's life at a very early age. In fact, he has joked that "ink was always in my blood. I don't remember it, of course, but as a baby in my mother's arms I used to visit my uncle's printing works on the narrow high street of our town. I used to point and grin and gurgle as the pages of the local newspaper rolled off the machines."

By the age of six or seven, Almond was spending a lot of his free time making up stories and putting them to paper. "I always knew I wanted to write," he recalled. "I used to write little books when I was a kid, and right through my childhood I wrote — obviously just bits and pieces, fragments, but it was always what I wanted to do." He also loved reading adventure tales, and was particularly fond of stories of King Arthur and the Knights of the Round Table.

"I always knew I wanted to write. I used to write little books when I was a kid, and right through my childhood I wrote — obviously just bits and pieces, fragments, but it was always what I wanted to do."

Almond believes that his surroundings nourished his early interest in writing. His family's home was located on a hill on the outskirts of Newcastle upon Tyne, and he recalls that the house's windows looked far out over the countryside. "From our windows, we looked out towards the city that packed the opposite bank, towards the distant sea, and even on clear days toward the hazy Cheviots [a range of low mountains on the border of England and Scotland] an eternity away. It was a place that had everything necessary for the imagination."

Almond also grew up in an environment where storytelling was a part of everyday life. "I grew up in a big extended Catholic family," he said. "I listened to the stories and songs at family parties. . . . I ran with my friends through the open spaces and the narrow lanes. We scared each other with ghost stories told in fragile tents on dark nights. We promised never-ending friendship and whispered of the amazing journeys we'd take together." Even church services fed Almond's fascination with storytelling. "I trembled at the images presented to us in church, at the awful threats and glorious promises made by black-clad priests with Irish voices," he said.

EDUCATION

Almond received his early education in the Newcastle upon Tyne school system. He confesses that he disliked school. But he is quick to add that he loved the local library, which he described as "a little square building in which I dreamed that books with my name on them would stand one day on the shelves."

Almond also enjoyed such extracurricular activities as football (known as soccer in the United States). He had limited talent, but he played the sport with a fierce joy. In fact, one of his favorite memories from childhood was a playoff football match that was played in a heavy rain. "I had blood trickling from my brow and I played my best game ever," he recalled proudly. "It was a semi-final and we won." After completing his schooling in Newcastle upon Tyne, Almond enrolled at the University of East Anglia, from which he graduated with honors.

"

"I grew up in a big extended Catholic family. I listened to the stories and songs at family parties. . . . I ran with my friends through the open spaces and the narrow lanes. We scared each other with ghost stories told in fragile tents on dark nights. We promised never-ending friendship and whispered of the amazing journeys we'd take together."

"

CAREER HIGHLIGHTS

As readers of young adult fiction are well aware, Almond's dream of seeing his own books on library shelves came true. His novels *Skellig* and *Kit's Wilderness* are tremendously popular in England, and he is now regarded as one of the finest writers of fiction for children and young adults today. But the author achieved this fame only after years of hard work.

Teaching Children with Learning Problems

Almond's first career was in teaching. He taught primary school and adult courses for various periods, but he spent the majority of his time as a teacher helping children with learning problems. Almond says that during his years as an educator, "one of the things I came to see more and more was that a lot of these children . . . had learning problems because they had never really been told stories when they were young. They had never kind of shared in stories. . . . I spent a lot of my teaching career working on stories with children who had special learning problems. And I saw the power of stories to really help them to enjoy school, to enjoy learning."

Almond's interest in writing remained strong during this period. He wrote short stories in his free time and explored different ideas for novels, hope-

ful that he might one day be able to earn his living as a writer. But over time he realized that the demands of the teaching profession left little time for him to sit down and write. "I realized I had to get serious about [writing]," he remembered.

Becoming an Author

In 1982 Almond made a dramatic decision. He quit his teaching job, sold his house, and moved into a commune —a small community of people that shares ownership of property—so that he could concentrate on his writing. Over the next several years his productivity soared, and in 1985 he published his first book of short stories, *Sleepless Nights.* Almond was proud of the collection, but it sold few copies despite several good reviews.

Almond left the commune after a few years, but his determination to support himself as a writer remained strong. In 1987 he accepted the managing editor position at an English fiction magazine called *Panurge.* The magazine did not have the financial resources to employ a staff, however, so Almond was forced to spend much of his time taking care of mailings and basic office paperwork. In 1993, after six "exciting and exhausting" years at *Panurge,* Almond left the magazine.

Almond says that the storyline for Skellig *just naturally flowed into his mind. "Before* Skellig, *I spent many years painstakingly putting together short stories and an unpublished novel. I used to worry about my small output.* Skellig *felt like a gift, a reward for all of this hard work."*

During his years at *Panurge,* Almond also continued to produce his own short stories. In addition, he completed his first novel after five years of labor. But when he tried to sell the book for publication, it was rejected by all 33 publishers he sent it to. Almond's failure to sell the novel was a big disappointment, but he did not let it destroy his confidence. "I went on writing," he said. "More stories, more publications, a few small prizes. Another novel, never finished. Another story collection was published, *A Kind of Heaven,* 12 years after the first. Then at last I started writing about growing up in our small . . . town: a whole sequence of stories, half-real, half-imaginary, that I called *Stories from the Middle of the World.*"

Childhood Memories Spark Creation of *Skellig*

Almond states that the stories he wrote about growing up in a northern England town were "very deliberately about me, about my sisters and my brother and my parents. They were about the things that had happened to us, some of which were tragic, some of which . . . were quite joyful." As

Almond tapped into his childhood memories, he says that he actually "adopted the mindset of a child, revisiting all the vividness of those places and experiences. Not long after that, *Skellig* came to me as if it had been waiting there to come out." The author remains convinced that he never would have been inspired to write *Skellig* if he had not spent so much time remembering the happy and sad events of his youth.

According to Almond, the first line of the award-winning novel *Skellig*—"I found him in the garage on Sunday afternoon"—just came to him out of the blue one morning. From there, the author claims that the rest of the storyline just naturally flowed into his mind. "Before *Skellig,* I spent many years painstakingly putting together short stories and an unpublished novel," said Almond. "I used to worry about my small output. *Skellig* felt like a gift, a reward for all of this hard work."

In the story, a boy named Michael and the rest of his family have just moved into an old, rundown house. A short time later, Michael discovers a frail, mysterious old man named Skellig in their garage. As the novel progresses, he and a bright and independent young neighbor girl named Mina try to unravel the mystery of Skellig, who has big angel-like wings and a strange link to a nearby family of wild owls. But as the youngsters nurse him back to health, Skellig's past and identity remain hazy. "As Skellig grows stronger and responds to the children's love and attention, he becomes more and more mysterious, and their time with him stranger and more magical," observed Perri Klass in the *New York Times Book Review.* Meanwhile, Michael's newborn infant sister is admitted into the hospital with a life-threatening heart condition. As the novel proceeds, Almond skillfully weaves these two storylines together into an exciting and powerful tale.

Praise for *Skellig*

When Almond completed *Skellig,* the book was accepted by the first publisher he approached. This immediate acceptance delighted and surprised the author, whose earlier novel had been rejected at every turn. But when *Skellig* was published in England in 1998, it became clear that the publisher that accepted Almond's book knew what it was doing. Though written for ages 9 to 12, *Skellig* was a huge hit with readers of all ages, and it received nearly unanimous praise from critics. *Five Owls* magazine, for example, called it a "novel of faith and hope" and a "book of rare spirituality for young adults." *Booklist* added that the novel was an "amazing work. Some of the writing takes one's breath away." It also won numerous awards, including two of Great Britain's biggest literary prizes, the Carnegie Medal and the Whitbread Children's Book of the Year Award. *Skellig* also became a bestseller in the United States after its publication here in 1999. It was named a Michael L. Printz Honor Book.

The astounding popularity of *Skellig* changed Almond's life forever. The novel's success gave him financial security that he had never enjoyed before. It also made him a celebrity in England and other parts of Europe. "The breakthrough with *Skellig* was great, and some people tried to describe me as an overnight success, but of course I'd already been writing for many years," commented Almond.

Almond found that his sudden fame also gave him an opportunity to voice his concerns about several education issues in England. For example, he spoke out against the growing emphasis on testing in English school systems (student testing has also been on the rise in the United States in recent years). Supporters of increased student testing say that it helps parents and administrators measure which schools are doing a good job of teaching their students. But Almond and other critics argue that too much testing takes the joy and creativity out of learning for children. "The testing of core subjects is important but schools need to strike a balance," wrote Almond. "The drive to improve [test scores] must not be at the expense of creative teaching and activities, so important to the learning process. . . . There is more to learning, and life, than just English, math, and science." In addition, Almond feels that too many adults underestimate the capabilities of children, whom he praises as "truly perceptive and creative readers."

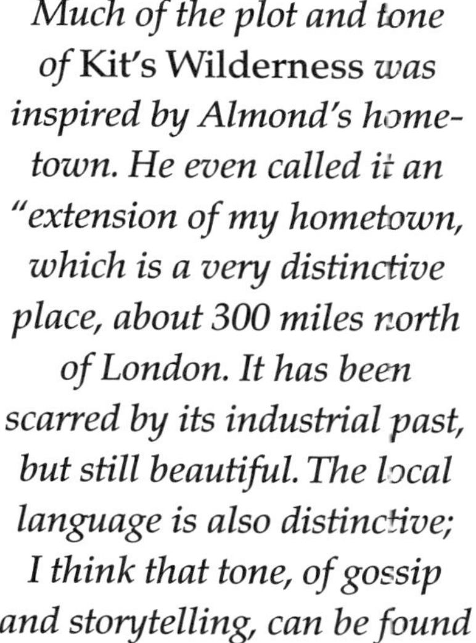

"

Much of the plot and tone of Kit's Wilderness *was inspired by Almond's hometown. He even called it an "extension of my hometown, which is a very distinctive place, about 300 miles north of London. It has been scarred by its industrial past, but still beautiful. The local language is also distinctive; I think that tone, of gossip and storytelling, can be found in my writing voice."*

"

Kit's Wilderness Draws New Fans

Almond's second novel for young readers, *Kit's Wilderness,* was published in 1999 in Great Britain (it was published one year later in the United States). Unlike *Skellig,* this book was written for teens. When *Kit's Wilderness* was released, the author said that much of its plot and tone was inspired by his

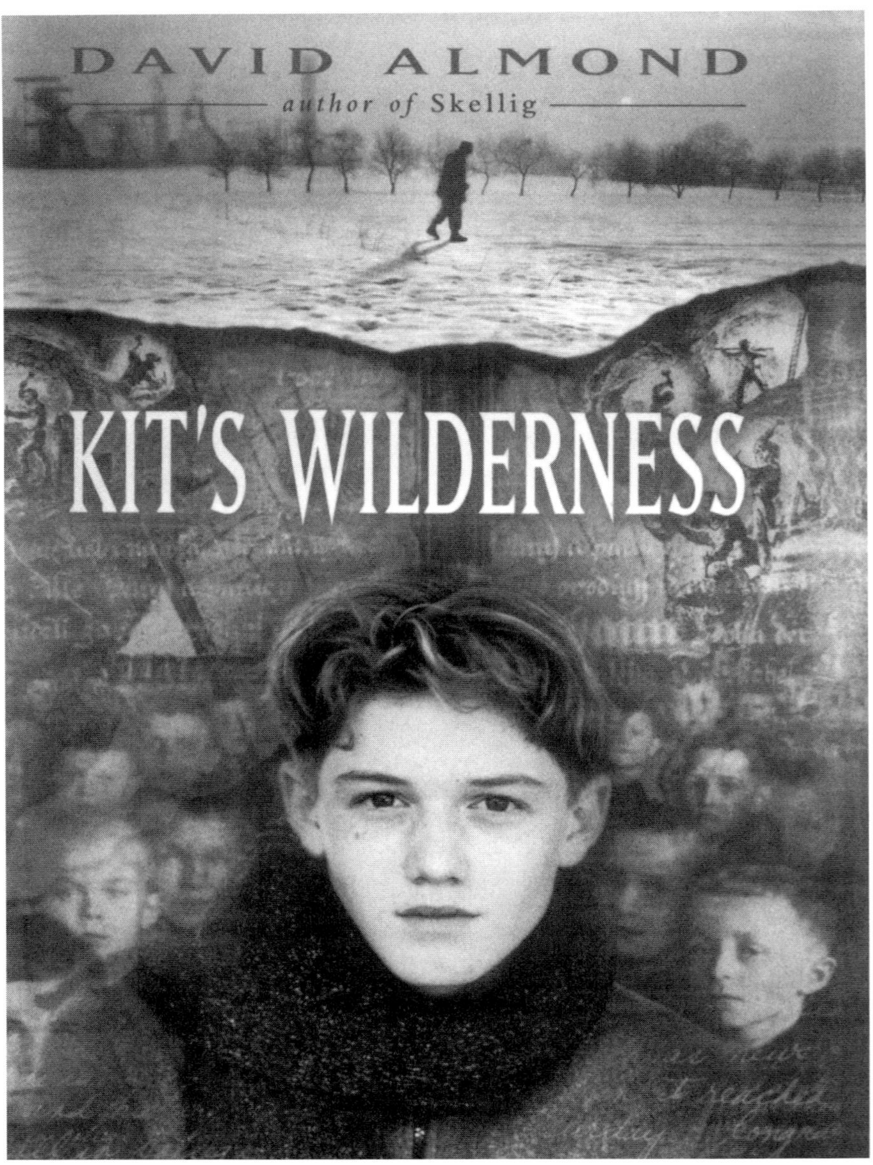

hometown. He even called it an "extension of my hometown, which is a very distinctive place, about 300 miles north of London. It has been scarred by its industrial past, but still beautiful. The local language is also distinctive; I think that tone, of gossip and storytelling, can be found in my writing voice."

Kit's Wilderness is narrated by the character of Kit Watson, a boy who becomes involved with other children in a make-believe game called "Death." This game requires chosen players to stay alone in an abandoned mine, the scene of a deadly coal mining accident that had killed several boys from town more than a century earlier. But when Kit is selected to stay in the mine, he actually sees the spirits of the boys who died. As the novel progresses, Kit's experiences with the ghosts lead him on a mission to save his sensitive friend Askew from a terrible family situation.

Almond wrote *Kit's Wilderness* for a slightly older audience than *Skellig,* but again readers of all ages loved it. Critics also praised the author's effort. *Publishers Weekly* stated that "he takes readers on a thrilling and spine-tingling ride." *Booklist* added that in *Kit's Wilderness,* Almond "created a heartbreakingly real world fused with magic realism."

"In lyrical fashion, Kit's story melds the darkness of the past with bright hope for the future. Almond creates a heartbreakingly real world fused with magic realism as he juggles several plot elements with dexterity. He also leads the reader to understanding how life can be seen through the prisms of space and time."
—Peter M. Butts, chair of the Michael L. Printz Award selection committee

Winning the Michael L. Printz Award

Acclaim for the book intensified in 2001, when *Kit's Wilderness* won the prestigious Michael L. Printz Award. The Printz Award is given by the American Library Association annually to a book that exemplifies literary excellence in young adult (YA) literature. Almond's work was generously praised by Peter M. Butts, chair of Printz Award selection committee. "In lyrical fashion, Kit's story melds the darkness of the past with bright hope for the future," said Butts. "Almond creates a heartbreakingly real world fused with magic realism as he juggles several plot elements with dexterity. He also leads the reader to understanding how life can be seen through the prisms of space and time."

When Almond accepted the award, he gave a speech to talk about the magic of literature. "When I was a boy, I roamed the little library in our little town. It was just down the street, just next to a battered patch of grass where I played soccer with my friends. I dreamed that one day I'd go back

into that library and see books with my name on them standing on the shelves, that my books would be there to be read by people of my town. That's happened now, of course. I've stood in the exact same place where I stood when I was 11 years old and put my hand up to the exact same bookshelf where I dreamed they'd be, and there they were, and that 11 year old boy is still inside of me. . . . What I like to imagine now is that as I stand here on the west coast of the [United States], a young boy or girl is standing in a little library in Felling-on-Tyne thousands of miles away. They take down my book. They read my name on the cover. They read the book and it infects them with their own dream, that one day they'll walk into the library, reach up to a shelf, and see a book not with David Almond's name, but with their own name printed on the cover."

In that same speech, Almond thanked many people for his award, but he especially thanked his readers. "How often do we hear young people stereotyped and dismissed? Oh, kids today. Don't they make you weep? Glued to TV and cell phones, brains plugged deep into the net. So shallow, rowdy, superficial. I'd like to drag the glib dismissers into the discussions I get into in classrooms. I'd like to show them the letters I get. I'd like them to see what writers and readers have always known, that the mysterious circuits of the human brain, no matter what its age, will always be set to spark by narrative and language."

"I don't see the world as a terrible place. I actually think the world is pretty miraculous. Writing for children, I almost feel a duty to pass on my sense of optimism. Joy just might triumph over tragedy."

Recent Work

In 2000 Almond published two books. One of these was *Counting Stars,* the collection of short stories that had first inspired Almond to write *Skellig* a few years earlier. The other was Almond's third novel for young adults, called *Heaven Eyes*. This novel tells the story of three parentless children who run away from an orphanage by floating a makeshift raft down a long river. During their journey they stop at an old printing factory, where they find two people living in the facility's abandoned offices. One is a young girl with webbed fingers and toes named Heaven Eyes. Her companion is an old caretaker whom she calls Grandpa. As the three orphans get to know the mysterious Heaven Eyes, they learn that she has what *School Library Journal* called the ability "to see through all the darkness, grief, and trouble in the world to the joy that lies beneath."

Just like Almond's two previous books, *Heaven Eyes* was warmly received by readers and reviewers in England and beyond. "Almond's vivid and original storytelling creates a very real sense of wonder," commented the

"

"These books are suffused with the landscape and spirit of my own childhood. By looking back into the past, by re-imagining it and blending it with what I see around me now, I found a way to move forward and to become something that I am intensely happy to be: a writer for children."

"

Christian Science Monitor. A reviewer for *School Library Journal,* meanwhile, described the novel as "powerful, lyrical, and enchanting."

Many readers of Almond's YA novels have commented that they are all about children who are searching for freedom from unhappy or difficult lives. In many cases, these children find comfort in natural settings or their interactions with wild or magical creatures. This theme reflects Almond's belief that wilderness areas can be places of emotional healing. "Children don't just want to play in the living room or the garden," he states. "They want to go out into places that are a little wilder. I think that we try to give children very packaged lives. . . . We try to teach and tame the natural wildness out of our children. I think that children recognize this. They see something wilder (which is not the same as 'out of control') in the natural world and are drawn to it. . . . Stories are crucial in helping us to grow up into people who are 'civilized' but who also recognize the importance of wilderness, in ourselves and in the world around us."

Almond also sees his stories as sources of hope for children. "I don't see the world as a terrible place. I actually think the world is pretty miraculous. Writing for children, I almost feel a duty to pass on my sense of optimism. Joy just might triumph over tragedy." Almond's interest in reaching children has also led him outside the world of novels. In 2000 he wrote his first play for children, called *Wild Girl, Wild Boy*. This drama premiered in London, England, in the spring of 2001.

Almond is grateful that his children's books are so widely read, in part because they have all been inspired so heavily by his own experiences as a youth. "These books are suffused with the landscape and spirit of my own childhood," he explained. "By looking back into the past, by re-imagining it and blending it with what I see around me now, I found a way to move forward and to become something that I am intensely happy to be: a writer for children."

MARRIAGE AND FAMILY

Almond is married to Sara Jane Palmer, a sculptor and ceramist. They have one daughter, named Freya Grace Almond-Palmer. The family lives in what Almond calls "a 90-year-old terraced house" in Newcastle upon Tyne, his hometown.

HOBBIES AND OTHER INTERESTS

Almond enjoys hiking in the hills and valleys around his home. He also enjoys reading and listening to music.

WRITINGS

Children's Books

Skellig, 1998 (published in the United States in 1999)
Kit's Wilderness, 1999 (published in the United States in 2000)
Heaven Eyes, 2000 (published in the United States in 2001)

Short Story Collections

Sleepless Nights, 1985
A Kind of Heaven, 1997
Counting Stars, 2000

HONORS AND AWARDS

Tyrone Guthrie Award: 1990
Junior Literary Guild Selection: 1998, for *Skellig*
Whitbread Children's Book of the Year Award: 1998, for *Skellig*
Carnegie Medal (Library Association): 1998, for *Skellig*
Smarties Prize: 1998, for *Skellig*

Smarties Silver Award: 1999, for *Kit's Wilderness*
Michael L. Printz Award: 2001, for *Kit's Wilderness*

FURTHER READING

Books

Something About the Author, Vol. 114, 2000

Periodicals

Book, May 2001, p.80
Booklist, Feb. 1, 1999, p.974; Jan. 1, 2000, p.898; Jan. 1, 2001, p.950; Apr. 1, 2001, p.1464
Christian Science Monitor, May 10, 2001, p.21
Five Owls, May-June 1999, p.110
Guardian (London), July 15, 1999, p.10
Horn Book Magazine, May 1999, p.326; Mar. 2000, p.192; Mar. 2001, p.205
Independent (London), July 15, 1999, p.3
New York Times Book Review, June 6, 1999, p.49
Publishers Weekly, Dec. 7, 1998, p.60; Jan. 3, 2000, p.77; Mar. 5, 2001, p.80
Reading Time, May 1999, p.25
School Library Journal, Mar. 2000, p.233; Mar. 2001, p.245; Apr. 2001, p.48
Times (London), July 15, 1999
USA Today, Aug. 5, 1999, p.D8
Washington Post, Aug. 20, 2000, p.X10

ADDRESS

Random House Children's Books
1540 Broadway
New York, NY 10036

WORLD WIDE WEB SITES

http://www.schoolsnet.com
http://www.achuka.co.uk/dase.htm
http://www.adhoc.co.uk/cambridge/bios
http://www.teenreads.com/authors/au-almond-david.asp

Joan Bauer 1951-

American Writer of Novels for Young Adults
Author of *Squashed, Thwonk, Rules of the Road,* and *Hope Was Here*

BIRTH

Joan Bauer was born on July 12, 1951, in River Forest, Illinois. Her parents were divorced when she was eight years old. From that time on, she was raised by her mother, Marjorie Good, who was a high school English teacher with a good sense of humor. She rarely saw her father, Theodore Baehler, whom she has described as "a very messed up man." Joan has two younger sisters, Karen and Barbara.

YOUTH

Growing up in Illinois, Bauer's main interest was comedy. She was fascinated with humor of all kinds, and she hoped to become a comedy writer someday. Her grandmother, who lived with her family, was a major influence in this area. She had once been a professional storyteller and often entertained her granddaughters with humorous tales. "She told stories of Norwegian immigrants who had just come to America and all the crazy things that happened to them adjusting to a new land," Bauer remembered. "Her influence on me was profound — she was so amazingly talented and funny. Being with her was like getting a one-woman show for free. I think that through her stories she helped me develop a keen sense of humor at a very early age."

"[My grandmother] told stories of Norwegian immigrants who had just come to America and all the crazy things that happened to them adjusting to a new land. Her influence on me was profound — she was so amazingly talented and funny. Being with her was like getting a one-woman show for free. I think that through her stories she helped me develop a keen sense of humor at a very early age."

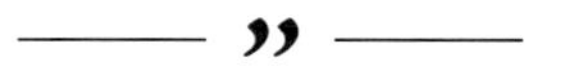

Sadly, Bauer's grandmother suffered from Alzheimer's disease, a progressive neurological disorder that slowly robs people of their memory and other functions. "One of the great tragedies of my grandmother's life was that she died of Alzheimer's disease," Bauer noted. "She lost her stories." Still, Bauer learned a great deal from her grandmother before she died. "She showed me the difference between derisive laughter that hurts others and laughter that comes from the heart," Bauer stated. "She showed me, too, that stories help us understand ourselves at a deep level."

Bauer enjoyed writing from an early age. She kept a diary throughout her childhood, and she also wrote a number of stories and poems. During her teen years, Bauer was slightly overweight and had only a few close friends. "I didn't always laugh at what my friends laughed at and they rarely giggled at my jokes," she recalled. "That, and the fact that I was overweight and very tall, all made me feel quite different when I was growing up — a bit like a water buffalo at a tea party." In her spare time, she worked at a series of odd jobs, including as a waitress, a receptionist, and an assistant typing teacher.

Throughout her youth, Bauer struggled to deal with a number of emotional issues involving her father. When she was 20, she finally confronted him about the damaging effects of his drinking, gambling, and abandoning the family. "I learned from that experience that there are times in life when we have choices—we can continue to be victims or we can move forward to be healthy people," she noted. Sadly, her father committed suicide a short time later. Bauer has called the day of her father's death "the saddest day of my life."

EDUCATION

Bauer attended elementary school in River Forest, then went to high school in Oak Park and Melrose Park, Illinois. Her school years were difficult ones for her, and she did not pursue a traditional path in her education. Upon completing high school, Bauer began working and did not attend college right away. She later took several college courses in journalism and screenwriting.

CAREER HIGHLIGHTS

As of 2001, Bauer has published six novels for young adults. She is known for writing humorous stories about offbeat characters. Many of her main characters are teenaged girls who are dealing with serious issues, like insecurity, low self-esteem, absent parents, and alcoholic family members. Yet each of her heroines manages to face her troubles with humor and hope for the future, and they usually end up winning in the end. As reviewer Tracey Firestone wrote in *School Library Journal,* "When it comes to creating strong, independent, and funny teenaged female characters, Bauer is in a class by herself."

Bauer often draws upon the struggles of her own youth in her writing. She hopes that her books can help today's teenagers work through similar problems. "Because so much was not positive for me, I want to write positive stories," she explained. "Because so much was painful for me, I want to show ways to overcome pain with emotional health, relationships, and humor. Because I desperately needed ties to my father, I write a great deal about complex fathers in my books. Because I never had a huge group of friends when I was growing up, I write about kids who tend to be loners."

Although Bauer's novels deal with serious issues, they also include healthy doses of humor. "It's easier for me to think and write funny because I really have a humorous outlook on life. I truly see humor as a way to get through life—it's an emotional tool for me. Humor helps me put difficult things in perspective. I see laughter as being a bridge between pain and redemption," she stated. "But, yes, it is hard to deal with serious, difficult things with a humorous touch. The primary rub for me is that I don't want anyone to think that I'm making fun of serious topics, like alcoholism or Alzheimer's disease."

"

"Because so much was not positive for me, I want to write positive stories. Because so much was painful for me, I want to show ways to overcome pain with emotional health, relationships, and humor. Because I desperately needed ties to my father, I write a great deal about complex fathers in my books. Because I never had a huge group of friends when I was growing up, I write about kids who tend to be loners."

Writing Her First YA Novel

In her 20s, Bauer worked in advertising sales for the *Chicago Tribune* and *Parade Magazine.* Although she built a good career for herself, she grew frustrated with the hectic pace and lack of creativity in her job. "I ended up with a few ulcers and was singularly miserable," she recalled. When she was about 30, she decided to try to earn a living as a free-lance writer. "I finally began to listen to my heart, quit my job, and started writing," she stated. "I wish I could say that everything started falling into place, but it was a slow, slow build—writing newspaper and magazine articles for not much money."

Bauer worked as a journalist for several years, then spent a brief time as a screenwriter. In the late 1980s, however, she was involved in a serious automobile accident. She suffered severe injuries to her back and neck that left her unable to sit at her desk for more than half an hour at a time. During her long recovery, she lost her screenwriting job because she was

not able to write screenplays fast enough to meet deadlines. With little else to do, Bauer finally began working on her first novel.

This book, called *Squashed,* tells the story of an overweight teenager named Ellie Morgan. Ellie is struggling to deal with the death of her mother and trying to earn the respect of her busy father. She becomes determined to grow the biggest, heaviest pumpkin in the county in order to win the coveted blue ribbon at the annual Harvest Fair. Bauer's trademark humor shows in the great lengths to which Ellie goes in nurturing her pumpkin, Max. "Not all vegetables are this draining," Ellie says. "Lettuce doesn't bring heartache. Turnips don't ask for your soul. Potatoes don't care where you are or even where they are. Tomatoes cuddle up to anyone who'll give them mulch and sunshine. But giants like Max need you every second. You can forget about a whiz-bang social life."

At first, Bauer had trouble finding a publisher for *Squashed.* But she eventually entered it in Delacorte's contest for first-time writers and won first prize. The book was published in 1992 and received positive reviews. For example, a *Publishers Weekly* reviewer called it "fast-paced and engrossing entertainment that startles the reader with its underlying strength."

Becoming a Popular YA Writer

Bauer followed the success of *Squashed* with several more well-regarded novels for young adults. Her second book, *Thwonk,* was published in 1995. It tells the story of Allison Jean (A.J.) McCreary, a teenager with a passion for photography. While on assignment to take a picture with a Valentine's Day theme for the school paper, A.J. finds a Cupid doll that comes to life and offers to grant her a wish. She asks for Cupid's help in attracting the attention of Peter Terris, the most handsome and popular boy in school. Once Peter falls in love with her and she is accepted by his popular friends, however, A.J. learns that romance and popularity are not as important as she thought. A *Publishers Weekly* reviewer noted that

"Bauer's buoyant narrative will elicit chuckles as it delivers its message (thwonk!) with the accuracy of a well-aimed arrow from Cupid."

Bauer published her third novel, *Sticks,* in 1996. In this book, the main character is a 10-year-old boy named Mickey Vernon. Mickey is fascinated with the game of pool and dreams of winning the annual tournament at his family's pool hall. In order to do so, however, he must beat the town bully. As the tournament approaches, Mickey learns the geometric strategy of the game and proves that a sharp mind is more valuable than big muscles. In general, critics were not as impressed with *Sticks* as they had been with Bauer's earlier efforts. For example, a reviewer for *Publishers Weekly* found the book "surprisingly sluggish" and commented that "fans of the light humor and breezy style of Bauer's earlier works are likely to be disappointed."

"Over the years, I have come to understand how deeply I need to laugh. It's like oxygen to me," she stated. "My best days as a writer are when I'm working on a book and laughing while I'm writing. Then I know I've got something."

Rules of the Road

Bauer returned to form with her fourth novel, *Rules of the Road,* published in 1998. *Rules of the Road* tells the story of 16-year-old Jenna Boller, whose father is an alcoholic. "My father was an alcoholic and the pain of that was a shadow that followed me for years," Bauer noted. "I attempted to address that pain in *Rules of the Road.* It was a very healing book for me." Like the characters in Bauer's other books, Jenna has an unusual passion in her life: selling shoes. "When I turned the rock over in my mind about what kind of a person would really succeed at selling shoes, it became clear to me that it would be the kind of person who was humble, not showy, didn't mind getting on her knees to help people," the author explained. "I wanted Jenna to have all of those attributes and to show how loving something ordinary can make it extraordinary."

In the novel, the elderly woman president of Gladstone Shoes recognizes Jenna's talent and ambition. She asks the teen, who has just received her driver's license, to drive her across the country for a stockholders' meeting. Along the way, Jenna learns that the woman is trying to save her company from a hostile takeover by her greedy son. Jenna also makes friends with a fellow shoe salesman who is a recovering alcoholic. When the salesman is tragically killed by a drunk driver, Jenna finds the courage to report her father for drunk driving. In a review for *Booklist,* Stephanie Zvirin called *Rules of the Road* "a warm, funny, insightful story about ordinary people who look beyond age to the things they have in common and the wisdom they can share." It received the *Los Angeles Times* Book Prize for Young Adult Fiction and the Golden Kite Award from the Society of Children's Book Writers and Illustrators.

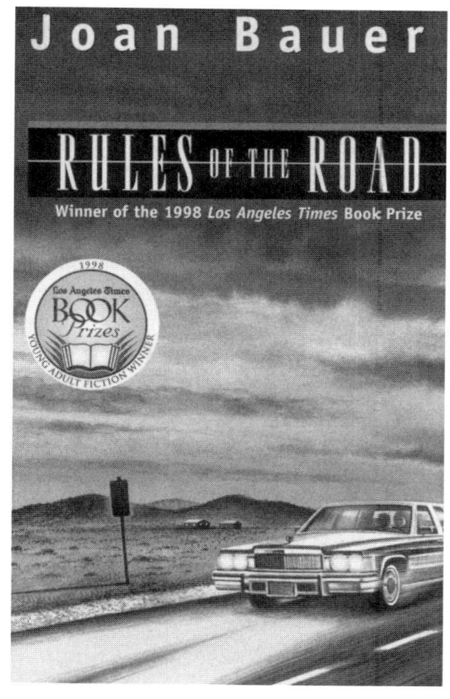

Backwater

Bauer's next book was *Backwater,* published in 1999. This novel tells the story of Ivy Breedlove, a 16-year-old girl from a wealthy family who is determined to pursue her love of history. She goes on a mission to find her long-lost aunt, a sculptor who has been living as a hermit in the Adirondack Mountains. Along the way, Ivy learns a lot about herself and her relationship with her family. "I love history—it links us to our past, present, and future. Sometimes it's thought of as kind of boring, but Ivy makes it come alive. So I took Ivy's talent and love and used them to build the plot and adventure of this story," Bauer explained. "What Ivy understands and learns in an even deeper way is that understanding history helps us to understand ourselves. She knows she is part of generations of people who have come before her—and she wants to understand what part of those ancestors are in her mind and emotions, too. People are who they are for many reasons—I think it's important for teenagers and for all of us to think about that."

Some critics complained that the plot of *Backwater* was farfetched, but others felt that young adult readers would enjoy the characters and action of the book. Sally Leahey of the *New York Times Book Review* commented that "Ivy never loses her common sense, her spunk, or her inquiring mind. There's an immediacy and sense of humor in her voice that will grab and hold the attention of teenage readers." Jean Franklin of *Booklist* added that "This warm, funny, patchwork quilt of a book offers a sturdy heroine, vivid characters, a touch of romance, and a final survival adventure that will keep readers turning pages to the last."

"

Bauer gives this advice to aspiring young writers. "Risk yourself on the pages. Don't be afraid to write about some of the rough things that have happened to you. That's when power streams in writing, when we've touched those links to pain and real life.... Write about things you care about—passion will carry you through when the work feels stuck. Listen to criticism, try to learn how to make things better. Don't be afraid to revise your work. . . . And don't forget to have fun, too. Let your heart go wild on the pages sometimes."

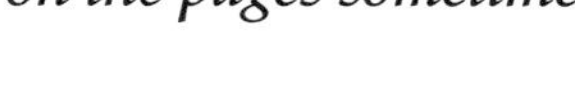

Hope Was Here

In 2000, Bauer published her most successful novel yet. *Hope Was Here* tells the story of Hope Yancey, a teenaged waitress from a broken family. Like Bauer's other heroines, Hope is strong, unique, sharp, and hard working. Hope lives with her Aunt Addie, who is a great short-order cook. They move from town to town across the country, working at various diners, until they finally land at the Welcome Stairways in rural Wisconsin. Before they know it, they become deeply involved with the town and its residents and decide to stay put. Hope finds romance in this warm and humorous story.

Hope Was Here was an immediate success with readers, spending several weeks on the best-seller lists. It was also a hit with critics, too, who were generous in their praise. J. Patrick Lewis of the *New York Times Book Review* said that Bauer's story "of a fatherless 16-year-old rings so clearly, it's as if the novel had been written by someone actually coming of age." Frances Bradburn of *Booklist* added that "Bauer's humor . . . makes the story rise above the rest, reinforcing the substantive issues of honesty, humanity, and the importance of political activism." *Hope Was Here* won the Christopher Award and was named a runner-up for the prestigious Newbery Medal. "Bauer juggles story lines as well as Hope juggles plates, and the lessons of waitressing expand into lessons about the essentials of life," said Caroline S. Parr, chair of the Newbery Award Selection Committee.

Advice for Aspiring Writers

Although Bauer enjoys her work as a writer, the process of writing is often difficult for her. She starts by doing a great deal of research about the topics that will be covered in her next book. In fact, she usually ends up with

huge stacks of library books covering the floor of her office. Next, she begins fleshing out characters, creating detailed life histories in order to understand their motivations. Her first draft is much more serious than the finished product and mostly includes the main action of the story. Bauer then revises over and over and gradually adds the humor that is found in all of her works. "Over the years, I have come to understand how deeply I need to laugh. It's like oxygen to me," she stated. "My best days as a writer are when I'm working on a book and laughing while I'm writing. Then I know I've got something."

"Girls, let me tell you something—so many of those photos of perfect, famous stars we see in magazines are fake. Those gorgeous faces and bodies have been retouched; pimples have been brushed away by computers; legs have been made prettier, hair shinier. We live in a world where we can't always trust the images that are being fed to us. And yet, it's so easy to look at those images and feel like we don't measure up. That's just not good."

Bauer is often asked to provide advice for aspiring young writers. "Risk yourself on the pages," she responds. "Don't be afraid to write about some of the rough things that have happened to you. That's when power streams in writing, when we've touched those links to pain and real life. Also, it's important to read quality writing, not junk. . . . Write about things you care about—passion will carry you through when the work feels stuck. Listen to criticism, try to learn how to make things better. Don't be afraid to revise your work. . . . And don't forget to have fun, too. Let your heart go wild on the pages sometimes."

The main focus of Bauer's novels is helping teenagers, especially girls, deal with some of the difficult aspects of growing up. She resents the way that society forces young women to try to live up to unrealistic standards, and she is careful to present her characters as real people with recognizable problems and insecurities. "Women have proved over the years that we can do just about anything in this world and do it well," Bauer stated. "But, I'm concerned by some of the ways girls are lied to in this society regarding their appearance. Girls, let me tell you something—so many of those photos of perfect, famous stars we see in magazines are fake. Those gorgeous faces and bodies have been retouched; pimples have been brushed away by computers; legs have been made prettier, hair shinier. We live in a world where we can't always trust the images that

School Library Journal, Nov. 2000, p.150
Teacher Librarian, Feb. 2000, p.60

ADDRESS

Putnam Publishing Group
200 Madison Ave.
New York, NY 10016

WORLD WIDE WEB SITES

http://www.joanbauer.com
http://www.teenreads.com/authors/au-bauer-joan.asp
http://jfg.girlscouts.org/readwritespeaklisten/enterviews/enterviews.htm
http://www.achuka.co.uk/guests/joanbsg.htm
http://www.penguinputnam.com/Author/AuthorPage

Kate DiCamillo 1964?-

American Writer of Novels for Young Adults
Author of *Because of Winn-Dixie* and *The Tiger Rising*

BIRTH

Kate DiCamillo was born in Philadelphia, Pennsylvania, around 1964. Her father left the family when she was five years old. From that time on, DiCamillo's mother, Betty, raised Kate and her older brother, Curt.

YOUTH

DiCamillo suffered a series of illnesses as a child. She had chronic pneumonia, which became worse during the winter.

Pneumonia is a disease in which the lungs fill up with fluid, making it difficult to breathe. But DiCamillo has said that being a sickly child was a blessing because it turned her into a reader. "I read everything I could get my hands on when I was a kid," she recalled. "And I loved it all. Some favorites were: *The 21 Balloons, The Secret Garden, The Yearling, Ribsy,* and a strange little book called *Somebody Else's Shoes.*"

Shortly after DiCamillo's father went away, her mother moved the family to a warmer climate in hopes of improving Kate's health. In 1969 they settled in Clermont, Florida, a small town located among the orange groves in the central part of the state, about 30 miles west of Orlando. The Florida weather did help DiCamillo get well, and she has many fond memories of her childhood in the South. "I grew up on a dead-end street with a wonderful neighborhood made up of kids and older people. I spent most of the year in my bare feet. I swam all the time. I had a wonderful dog named Nanette. The Cooper Memorial Library kept me in books. My mother read to me. I felt safe and loved. It was, in many respects, a wonderful childhood," she noted. "For me, as a writer, growing up in Florida was a wonderful gift. I absorbed that Southern cadence which I wouldn't have had access to otherwise, and it's a great voice for storytelling."

“

"I grew up on a dead-end street with a wonderful neighborhood made up of kids and older people. I spent most of the year in my bare feet. I swam all the time. I had a wonderful dog named Nanette. The Cooper Memorial Library kept me in books. My mother read to me. I felt safe and loved. It was, in many respects, a wonderful childhood. For me, as a writer, growing up in Florida was a wonderful gift. I absorbed that Southern cadence which I wouldn't have had access to otherwise, and it's a great voice for storytelling."

DiCamillo has always loved dogs. While she was growing up, she had a standard poodle that she used to dress up in an "old glittery green tutu." During her college years, she adopted an abused dog from the pound and turned its life around. She has said that the dog in her award-winning novel *Because of Winn-Dixie* is a combination of all the dogs she has known and loved in her life.

EDUCATION

DiCamillo attended the public schools in Clermont. She attended several colleges, including Rollins College and the University of Central Florida, before settling at the University of Florida in Gainesville. She earned a bachelor's degree in English in the mid-1980s.

DiCamillo started out by writing for an hour per day, five days per week. A short time later, she changed her writing goal to two pages per day. "I write every morning, or try to, no matter where I am or what I am doing. I give myself a page limit. Two pages. That's all I ask of myself. I never want to write, but I'm always glad that I have done it."

CAREER HIGHLIGHTS

After graduating from college, DiCamillo worked at a series of odd jobs. One of her most memorable work experiences was at Disney World. "I was too short to be Mickey Mouse and too tall to be a dwarf so, basically, I just told people to watch your step," she remembered. "It was great, good fun." In 1990, DiCamillo learned that one of her close friends was moving to Minneapolis, Minnesota. Almost on a whim, she decided to go along and make a fresh start in a new city. She has called her decision to move 1,500 miles north "my pre-mid-life crisis."

Becoming a Writer

Both during and after college, DiCamillo had often referred to herself as a writer. She always enjoyed writing stories, but she never devoted the time necessary to publish her work. Once she moved to Minneapolis, she discovered that the city was home to a large community of writers and artists. In 1993, she began attending meetings of a writers' group and set aside some time for writing. "It occurred to me that if I'm going to be a writer, I'm going to have to write," she noted. DiCamillo started out by writing for an hour per day, five days per week. A short time later, she changed her writing goal to two pages per day. "I write every morning, or try to, no matter where I am or what I am doing. I give myself a page limit. Two pages. That's all I ask of myself," she stated. "I never want to write, but I'm always glad that I have done it." Over the next few years, DiCamillo published a few adult short stories in magazines.

During this time, DiCamillo began working for the Bookman, a Minneapolis book distributor. Since her job was on the children's floor, she was exposed to a wide variety of children's books. Before long, she decided to focus on writing stories for children. "I always wanted to write and to tell stories," she recalled. "But I didn't start working on children's books until I got a job at a book warehouse on the children's floor. When I started reading some of the books, I was so impressed and moved that I decided I wanted to try it, too." DiCamillo particularly enjoyed the work of such authors as Karen Hesse, Katherine Paterson, and Patricia MacLachlan. She has said that the two books that most influenced her own young adult novels were *The Watsons Go to Birmingham—1963* by Christopher Paul Curtis and *Belle Prater's Boy* by Ruth White. (For information on these authors, see Hesse in *Biography Today Author Series,* Vol. 5; see Paterson in *Biography Today Author Series,* Vol. 3; see MacLachlan in *Biography Today Author Series,* Vol. 2; and see Curtis in *Biography Today Author Series,* Vol. 4, and Update in 2000 Cumulation.)

DiCamillo enjoyed working at the Bookman. But she struggled to pay her bills on her modest salary, and her long work weeks made it hard for her to fit in her daily writing sessions. In 1998, though, her circumstances changed when she received a grant from the McKnight Foundation—an organization that provides money to support and encourage talented writers. "The McKnight grant was life-changing," she remembered. "Before that, it was a hand-to-mouth existence. It was, 'Oh, God, don't let the car not start.' It allowed me to focus on writing." Later that year, DiCamillo met a sales representative for the Candlewick children's book publishing house at the annual Bookman Christmas party. She cornered the woman and gave her a manuscript for a picture book to pass along to an editor. "The poor woman was pregnant, had a cold, and had her toddler with her and I wouldn't let her go," she admitted.

"I always wanted to write and to tell stories. But I didn't start working on children's books until I got a job at a book warehouse on the children's floor. When I started reading some of the books, I was so impressed and moved that I decided I wanted to try it, too."

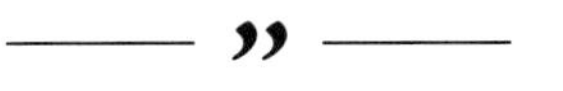

Candlewick rejected DiCamillo's first attempt at writing for children, but the editor who read her manuscript encouraged her to keep trying. A short time later, DiCamillo sent along a manuscript for a young adult novel. "Perseverance is the one word you could use to sum me up," she noted. This manuscript—about a girl whose life changes when she adopts a mangy dog—got lost for a while when the editor who was handling it left the company. But another editor eventually discovered it and decided that it was very promising. DiCamillo completed a series of rewrites of her book over the next two years. "That was scary," she admitted. "I did three to four rewrites and at first I thought, 'I baked a cake and now you're telling me to add three eggs.'" Her hard work finally paid off when her first novel, *Because of Winn-Dixie,* was published in 2000.

Because of Winn-Dixie

Because of Winn-Dixie tells the story of ten-year-old India Opal Buloni. Opal has just moved to Naomi, Florida, with her father, who is a preacher at the Open Arms Baptist Church. Opal's mother left the family when she was a toddler, and both Opal and her father still feel hurt, lonely, and

abandoned. At first, Opal struggles to make friends in the new town. But everything changes when she finds a mangy dog in the produce aisle of the local supermarket and brings him home. "My name is India Opal Buloni, and last summer my daddy, the preacher, sent me to the store for a box of macaroni-and-cheese, some white rice, and two tomatoes and I came back with a dog," the story begins. "Mostly, he looked like a big piece of old brown carpet that had been left out in the rain." The dog—which

"

Unlike many stories she has written, Because of Winn-Dixie *came to DiCamillo very easily—almost like the book wrote itself. "I don't want to sound nuts or anything, but this is the way it really happened: One night before I went to sleep, I heard this little girl with a Southern accent say, 'I have a dog named Winn-Dixie.' When I woke up the next morning, the voice was still talking, and I started writing down what India Opal Buloni was telling me. Nothing I've written before or since has come so easily. It was, from beginning to end, pure pleasure."*

"

she names Winn-Dixie after the supermarket—draws Opal out of her shell and helps her build friendships with eccentric characters throughout the community.

DiCamillo came up with the idea for *Because of Winn-Dixie* in 1997, during one of the coldest winters on record in Minneapolis. As the temperature outside hovered around 30 degrees below zero for weeks, she found herself missing the warmth of Florida. "I was homesick. You couldn't walk outside without slipping on the ice and cracking your head. And I was missing the sound of Southern people talking. And I was missing having a dog," she explained. "My apartment building does not allow dogs. But imaginary dogs aren't against the rules. So I made one up." DiCamillo has described the novel as "a hymn of praise to dogs, friendship, and the South."

Unlike many stories she has written, *Because of Winn-Dixie* came to DiCamillo very easily—almost like the book wrote itself. "I don't want to sound nuts or anything, but this is the way it really happened: One night before I went to sleep, I heard this little girl with a Southern accent say, 'I have a dog named Winn-Dixie,'" she remembered. "When I woke up the next morning, the voice was still talking, and I started writing down what India Opal Buloni was telling me. Nothing I've written before or since has come so easily. It was, from beginning to end, pure pleasure."

Because of Winn-Dixie earned rave reviews and became a best-seller. Readers and critics alike found DiCamillo's story about Opal and her dog heartwarming and funny. "Winn-Dixie is the mangiest, most lovable pup you will meet in fiction, a dog with an abundance of personality and a smile so wide it makes him sneeze," Sue Corbett wrote in the *Miami Herald*. "Not much happens in Naomi, but what does happen to Opal and her dog is quietly, but exquisitely, rendered by DiCamillo. This is a rare book for young readers that is both intelligent and laugh-out-loud funny." Writing in *School Library Journal,* Helen Foster James added that "This well-crafted, realistic, and heart-warming story will be read and reread as a new favorite deserving a long-term place on library shelves."

An Award-Winning First Novel

DiCamillo won several awards for her first novel, including the Parent's Choice Gold Award. Before long, her publisher and some magazines began talking about *Because of Winn-Dixie* as a candidate for the Newbery Medal, which is the highest honor in children's literature. DiCamillo tried not to listen to the rumors, but she admitted that she had trouble sleeping the night before the award was announced. "It was like Christmas Eve when I still believed in Santa Claus," she recalled. "I'd try to sleep and wake up and it'd be two o'clock, and I'd think, 'How could it be only two o'clock?'" DiCamillo nearly hit the roof when her phone rang early the next morning. She learned that her novel had been named a Newbery Honor Book—a runner-up for the prestigious Newbery Medal. She was so excited that she could barely contain herself. "Someone from the committee called and told me and I said, 'Oh, my God, oh, my God, oh, my God,'" she remembered. "And then, to impress them with the extent of my verbal verbosity, I said, 'Thank you, thank you, thank you.' That was the entire conversation." After she hung up the phone, DiCamillo says, "I cried like a baby on the kitchen floor. Because . . . I used to go to the library and look for those books with the Newbery seal on them. And I couldn't believe my first book would win such an honor. I cried because I was so happy. And then my phone started ringing and it just rang all day."

Winning the Newbery Honor for her first young adult novel was quite a thrill for DiCamillo. It convinced her that the hard work of writing was worthwhile. "When I was writing it, I'd get up at four a.m. so I could write

"

After hearing about her Newbery Honor, DiCamillo says, "I cried like a baby on the kitchen floor. . . . I used to go to the library and look for those books with the Newbery seal on them. And I couldn't believe my first book would win such an honor. I cried because I was so happy. And then my phone started ringing and it just rang all day."

before I had to go to work and I'd wonder, "What am I doing? I might as well buy a lottery ticket.' But I won the lottery. That's what it feels like," she explained.

The Tiger Rising

Even before *Because of Winn-Dixie* was published, DiCamillo began working on her second novel, *The Tiger Rising,* which appeared in 2001. *The Tiger Rising* tells the story of Rob Horton, a 12-year-old boy who moves to the small town of Lister, Florida, six months after his mother dies of cancer. He lives with his emotionally distant father at the Kentucky Star Motel, where his father also works. Ever since his father slapped him for crying at his mother's funeral, Rob has tried to suppress all of his feelings. He develops a way of "not-thinking" about unpleasant things, like his mother's death, the itchy rash on his legs, and the bullies who pick on him at school. "He imagined himself as a suitcase that was too full," DiCamillo writes in the novel. "He made all his feelings go inside the suitcase; he stuffed them in tight and then sat on the suitcase and locked it shut."

One morning, Rob goes walking in the woods behind the hotel and finds a tiger in a cage. That same day, he meets a new girl named Sistine Bailey on the school bus. Sistine feels very angry and bitter about her parents' recent divorce, and she expresses her volatile emotions freely. The two young people become friends, and they eventually decide to set the tiger free. Their decision has shocking and tragic results, but it also helps Rob express his emotions and begin to heal. DiCamillo noted that the story "is about what happens when you share your heart with somebody else; and it is also about the danger of keeping things locked up." She described it as "considerably darker [than *Because of Winn-Dixie*], but there's light and redemption in it."

Like her first novel, DiCamillo came up with the idea for *The Tiger Rising* in an unusual way. "Rob, the main character, showed up in a short story I wrote and then hung around the house driving me crazy. I finally asked him what he wanted, and he told me he knew where there was a tiger," she recalled. "Concurrently, Florida got a lot of rain. One of the cages at the zoo had flooded, and I still don't understand how this could work, but it flooded to the point that a tiger got out. And I thought, 'A tiger and Rob, a beaten-down boy. What happens when those two things intersect?' Things just kind of progressed from there."

Though it did not receive the same level of attention as *Because of Winn-Dixie,* DiCamillo's second book for young adults received positive reviews. "This slender story is lush with haunting characters and spare descriptions, conjuring up vivid images," reviewer Kit Vaughn wrote in *School Library Journal.* "It deals with the tough issues of death, grieving, and the great accompanying sadness, and has enough layers to embrace any reader." Writing in the *New York Times,* Linnea Lannon noted that the author "again explores the difficulty of fitting into a new place. But *The Tiger Rising* is even more emotionally affecting as Rob and Sistine, united by their aloneness, grapple with unlocking their own heartaches as they debate whether to free the tiger."

Success Keeps Her Busy

Ever since DiCamillo won the Newbery Honor for *Because of Winn-Dixie,* her life has been a whirlwind of book signings and school visits. "I'm busier now than I ever imagined I would be; but I feel blessed in that I have found what I am supposed to be doing with my life," she said. "It's wonderful to tell stories and have people listen to them." DiCamillo has particularly enjoyed meeting young fans and answering their questions. "They want to know everything—how I make up names, which hand I write with, the right or left, if I had a dog when I was a kid, if I'm married, practical advice on how to get a book published," she recalled.

DiCamillo claims that, in some ways, achieving such great success with her first book has made it more difficult for her to write. Now that she knows it is very likely that people will read her work, she feels pressure not to disappoint her readers. "Before, I knew full well I was hitting my head against a brick wall," she noted. "Now when I sit down to write, there's a Greek chorus behind me: 'This isn't like *Winn-Dixie*' or 'She's writing the same thing over and over.'" But DiCamillo has come up with some strategies to deal with her nerves. "I get up really early, when my brain is fuzzy enough," she explained. "Then I'm not thinking of the reader, the critic, the media—I'm just writing."

Some readers of both *Because of Winn-Dixie* and *The Tiger Rising* have noticed that the main characters in both books have lost their mothers. She says that writing the books helped her come to terms with the loss of her father, and she hopes that her work will give strength to young people who are dealing with the same issues. "My father left us when I was five years old. I think I bring that loss to bear on every story I tell," she stated. "At the same time, I have been blessed with wonderful, true friends. I have found, in my own life, that sorrow and loss seem to be counter-balanced with joy and love. I think that 'emotional equation' is always present in my mind when I am writing."

"My father left us when I was five years old. I think I bring that loss to bear on every story I tell. At the same time, I have been blessed with wonderful, true friends. I have found, in my own life, that sorrow and loss seem to be counter-balanced with joy and love. I think that 'emotional equation' is always present in my mind when I am writing."

On Writing

When she talks about her reasons for writing, DiCamillo often quotes E.B. White, the author of the children's classic *Charlotte's Web*. "E.B. White said, 'All that I hope to say in books, all that I ever hope to say, is that I love the world.' That's the way I feel, too," she stated. She tells aspiring young writers to pay attention to the world around them in order to find inspiration for their writing. "What stories are hiding behind the faces of the people that you walk past every day? What love? What hopes? What despair?" she said. "What I discovered is that every time you look at the world and the people in it closely, lovingly, imaginatively, it changes you. The world, under the microscope of your attention, opens up like a beautiful, strange flower and gives itself back to you in ways you could never imagine. . . . Writing is seeing the world. It is paying attention."

HOME AND FAMILY

DiCamillo is not married and does not have children. She continues to live in Minneapolis, where she works at a children's used bookstore.

SELECTED WRITINGS

Because of Winn-Dixie, 2000
The Tiger Rising, 2001

HONORS AND AWARDS

McKnight Artist Fellowship for Writers: 1998
Parent's Choice Gold Award (Parent's Choice Foundation): 2000, for *Because of Winn-Dixie*
Josette Frank Award (Bank Street College of Education Children's Book Committee): 2000, for *Because of Winn-Dixie*
Notable Book Award (*New York Times*): 2000, for *Because of Winn-Dixie*
Best Children's Book of the Year (*Publishers Weekly*): 2000, for *Because of Winn-Dixie*
Book Sense Book of the Year Award (American Booksellers Association): 2001, for *Because of Winn-Dixie*

FURTHER READING

Periodicals

Horn Book, July 2000, p.455; May 2001, p.321
Jacksonville Florida Times-Union, Apr. 9, 2001, p.C1
Miami Herald, July 6, 2000; Feb. 27, 2001, p.A4
Minneapolis Star-Tribune, Feb. 28, 2001, p.E1
New York Times, June 3, 2001, p.49
New York Times Book Review, May 14, 2000, p.26
Orlando Sentinel, Sep. 10, 2001, p.4 (Lake Sentinel sec.); Sep. 28, 2001, p.E1
Publishers Weekly, Feb. 21, 2000, p.88; June 26, 2000, p.30; Jan. 15, 2001, p.77
School Library Journal, June 2000, p.143; Mar. 2001, p.246

ADDRESS

Candlewick Press
2067 Massachusetts Avenue
Cambridge, MA 02134

WORLD WIDE WEB SITES

http://www.candlewick.com
http://childrensbooks.about.com/library/weekly/aa040801a.htm
http://www.teenreads.com
http://www.bnkst.edu/bookcommittee/speeches/00_josette_dicamillo.html

Jack Gantos 1951-

American Writer of Books for Children and Young Adults
Author of the "Rotten Ralph" Series, the "Jack Henry" Series, and the "Joey Pigza" Books

BIRTH

John Bryan Gantos, Jr.—better known as Jack—was born on July 2, 1951, in Mount Pleasant, Pennsylvania. His father, John Gantos, Sr., was a construction supervisor. His mother, Elizabeth (Weaver) Gantos, stayed home to take care of Jack, his brother Alex, and his two sisters, Karen and Betsy.

that they had to part with him because they were moving overseas. As it turned out, however, the couple only pretended to be leaving the country because they were desperate to get rid of their ill-mannered cat.

So Gantos began writing children's stories about his cat. Several of these stories were eventually published in the author's popular "Rotten Ralph" series, which was illustrated by his friend Nicole Rubel. The first book in the series, *Rotten Ralph,* was published in 1976—the same year Gantos earned his bachelor of fine arts degree in creative writing from Emerson. "I was the darling of the English writing department because I'd actually published books," he noted. Over the next few years, Gantos worked as a free-lance writer and continued publishing picture books. He also worked part-time at Emerson as a creative writing instructor and continued taking classes. He earned a master of arts degree in 1984.

CAREER HIGHLIGHTS

In his 25-year career as a writer, Jack Gantos has published more than 30 books. He first became well-known as the author of humorous picture books for children ages four through eight. Some of his most popular books feature Rotten Ralph, the trouble-making cat who still manages to find a place in the heart of his patient owner, a little girl named Sarah. After concentrating on picture books for many years, Gantos branched out into writing books for middle-grade readers in the 1990s. His youthful journals form the basis of the autobiographical stories in the "Jack Henry" series. He has also published two award-winning books about Joey Pigza, a boy who struggles with Attention Deficit Hyperactivity Disorder (ADHD). ADHD is condition that makes it difficult for sufferers to concentrate, sit still, or control their impulses.

Throughout his career, critics have praised Gantos for understanding the sort of stories that appeal to children. His books include outrageous humor and exaggerated elements, but they also feature positive values and meaningful messages about the difficulties of growing up. Gantos—who spent much of his own adolescence watching others from the sidelines as "the new kid"—says that the overall theme of his books is "the outsider as hero. The outsider as free thinker. The outsider who is true to his insides."

The "Rotten Ralph" Series

As of 2001, Gantos had published 15 books about Rotten Ralph and Sarah, the young girl who continually forgives his bad behavior. Over the years, Ralph manages to ruin Sarah's Halloween, Christmas, Thanksgiving, and

many other events with his naughty antics. For example, Ralph puts goldfish into the punch bowl at a party, and he dumps his old cat food into children's trick-or-treat bags at Halloween. But Sarah loves Ralph anyway. "He gets carried away, he gets in over his head, he loses control," Gantos said of his famous cat. "He's kind of like a four-year-old, where he knows a little better, but he just gets caught up in the moment. . . . I think where kids really empathize with the character is that he's loved, right or wrong. Unbeknownst to me (at the time), that is a very powerful message."

In *Rotten Ralph's Show and Tell,* published in 1989, Ralph manages to ruin everything Sarah plans to take to school and show her classmates. He pastes her stamp collection all over his fur, and he uses her violin like a bow and arrow. Then, when Sarah takes Ralph to school for show and tell as a last resort, he embarrasses her in front of the class. Writing in *Parenting,* Leonard S. Marcus called the book "a devilishly witty fable about childish mischief-making and unconditional love."

In *Not So Rotten Ralph,* published in 1994, Sarah finally gets fed up with her feline companion and sends him to kitty obedience school to learn some manners. The rules at the school prohibit meowing, hissing, burping, begging, sneakiness, and having fun. In one exercise, Ralph must keep his paws to himself in a room full of fragile objects. When Sarah finally arrives to collect him, Ralph is a changed kitty. But Sarah soon begins to miss the old Ralph, and she actually tempts him to misbehave in order to get her naughty cat back. Writing in *Booklist,* Stephanie Zvirin said that the book "not only sparkles with the usual Ralph pranks, but also gives the feisty feline a little payback of sorts for a change."

"

"He gets carried away, he gets in over his head, he loses control," Gantos said of Ralph, his famous cat. "He's kind of like a four-year-old, where he knows a little better, but he just gets caught up in the moment. . . . I think where kids really empathize with the character is that he's loved, right or wrong. Unbeknownst to me (at the time), that is a very powerful message."

In Gantos's 1997 addition to the series, *Rotten Ralph's Rotten Romance,* Ralph gets angry when he is forced to attend a Valentine's Day party. He tries everything to sabotage the event, including rubbing his fur with garbage, smearing dog food on his lips so no one will kiss him, and bringing a gift box of chocolate that is full of ants. "It's no wonder kids love Ralph—what a perfect vicarious way to get back at all those well-meaning adults who make you go to boring parties where everyone else seems to be having a great time," Elizabeth S. Watson wrote in *Horn Book.*

And in *Back to School for Rotten Ralph,* published in 1998, Sarah is excited by the start of the new school year and the opportunity to make new friends. But the troublesome kitty gets jealous and makes a tricky plan to go to school with Sarah, in disguise, and sabotage her new friendships. But his plan is soon exposed, his identity is revealed, and the entire class wants to be friends with Sarah and Ralph. "Gantos and Rubel have collaborated to create another wickedly funny adventure about a cat so rambunctiously rotten that you've just gotta love him," reviewer Michael Cart wrote in *Booklist.* By 1999, the books had become so popular that some of the "Rotten Ralph" stories were turned into an animated series for the Fox Family Channel.

The "Jack Henry" Series

In the mid-1990s, Gantos changed the focus of his writing from picture books to books for middle-grade readers. His work for this audience includes four books about Jack Henry, a boy who struggles to fit in because his family moves to a new city every year. Gantos based these books on the journals he had kept during junior high and high school. "I wrote the stories based on real things that happened to me," he noted. "I had written them down in my diary and now I've rewritten them."

The first book in the "Jack Henry" series, *Heads or Tails: Stories from the Sixth Grade,* was published in 1994. It is a collection of autobiographical stories, written in diary form. The main character, Jack, is a sixth-grader who has lived in nine houses and attended five schools because his father is always moving the family around in his search for a better job. Although Jack wants to do the right thing, strange things seem to happen and he often finds himself in trouble. For example, when Jack forgets to put away his bike, a hurricane blows in and carries it away. "The stories are whimsical, low key, and appealing, largely because of their real-life quality," Elizabeth S. Watson wrote in *Horn Book.* "This is what it's really like to survive sixth grade."

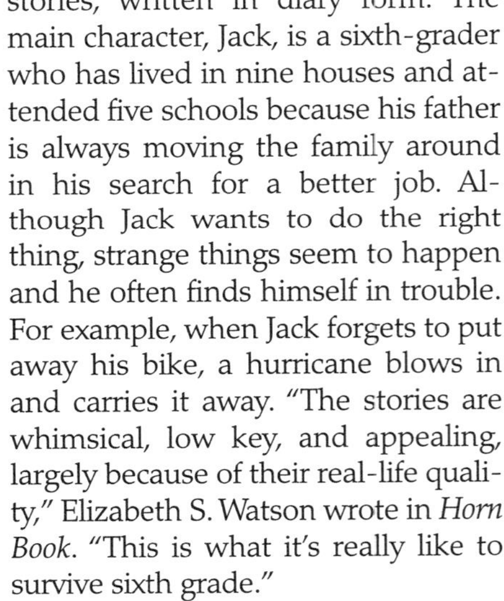

> *Gantos based the "Jack Henry" books on the journals he had kept during junior high and high school. "I wrote the stories based on real things that happened to me. I had written them down in my diary and now I've rewritten them."*

The second book in the series, *Jack's New Power: Stories from a Caribbean Year* (1995), follows Jack and his family to the island of Barbados, where Jack attends seventh grade. He returns to Florida for eighth grade in the third book in the series, *Jack's Black Book* (1997). In this collection of stories, Jack buys a new black notebook and plans to fill the pages by writing a brilliant novel. When he has trouble getting started, he goes in search of strange, funny, and even humiliating experiences so that he will have something to write about.

Jack on the Tracks: Four Seasons of the Fifth Grade (1999) is a prequel to the other books in the series. As a fifth grader, Jack is fascinated with strange and disgusting things, like watching his father eat a 72-ounce steak. He also tries without success to get on his teacher's good side, and conducts dangerous experiments on the nearby train tracks. Writing in *Booklist,*

a zero-to-six year prison sentence for drug smuggling. While there, he meets a talented Elvis impersonator. Upon their release, Jakes becomes the other ex-convict's agent and is betrayed by him. Gantos has said that he wrote the novel as a way to come to terms with his time behind bars. "Yes, there is some sort of redemptive desire to write this material and get it out," he stated. "I don't think the material is necessarily saying . . . nobody please follow in my footsteps. This is not an essay. But it is a book which shows very baldly what happens if you make these kinds of decisions."

In his school presentations, Gantos says, "My objective is to teach children how to write like professional writers—how to find ideas, develop characters, come up with great action lines, and then to format it all so that it's structured like a professional story. Good creative writing is a marriage between great creativity and great structure. I want kids and teachers to know that a story has a beginning, a middle, and an end, and that creativity isn't just a free-for-all, a time for students to do anything they wish. Structure isn't going to stop creativity; rather, it gives creativity form."

Teaching Others to Write

Throughout his career as a writer, Gantos has also worked as a teacher of creative writing. He started out as a part-time instructor at Emerson College shortly after he earned his bachelor's degree. Over the years, he became a professor of creative writing and literature and started up a master's degree program in children's book writing at Emerson. He also spent semesters at several other colleges and universities as a visiting professor. In 1996, Gantos retired from teaching and moved to New Mexico. He decided to spend more time writing and presenting workshops and seminars.

Gantos particularly enjoys visiting with his young fans at elementary and middle schools. He visits between 40 and 50 schools across the United States each year. He is known for his outstanding presentations, which include lots of humorous stories as well as detailed instructions on how students can develop their creative writing skills. "My objective is to teach children how to write like professional writers—how to find ideas, develop characters, come up with great action lines, and then to format it all so that it's structured like a professional story," he explained. "Good creative writing is a marriage between great creativity and great structure. I want kids and teachers to know that a story has a beginning, a middle, and an end, and that creativity isn't just a free-for-all, a time for students to do anything they wish. Structure isn't going to stop creativity; rather, it gives creativity form."

"When I examine my life as a professional writer, I can say without a doubt that starting that first journal was the most important step in my career. I hope all of you get journals or diaries and get busy writing about all the interesting things that happen in your lives. Remember, a lot of people think that the 'good stuff' to write about always happens to somebody else. But I believe that the 'good stuff' is always happening to you. Believe this, and you will always have the courage to write something other people want to read."

As another way of connecting with young readers, Gantos agreed to publish two of his stories in serial form in newspapers across the country in 1999. He hoped that kids, and their parents, would enjoy reading the stories during the summer months. "I'm a big literacy advocate and when you get parents and children reading the same thing, that's when you get kids really excited about literature," he noted. "If I was a kid, it would be the kind of thing I would dig—having a story in the newspaper." Gantos believes that getting kids to read is ultimately more important than what they read. "I just hope that children read lots of books, mine or not, and develop a life of the mind and imagination that allows them the confidence to learn on their own what they need to know," he stated.

At the same time, Gantos takes his responsibility as an author of books for children very seriously. "The notion of writing for children is the same as the notion to write *War and Peace.* Writing good books for children is the same as writing good books for anyone," he noted. "[Children] are far greater readers than adults. They read more. They enjoy books. And books have a great impact on their lives. The written word does not roll off their backs like water off a duck. Instead the written word becomes a river of experience that courses through their imaginations, and ultimately adds to what they think, who they become, and why."

Advice to Young Writers

When giving advice to young writers, Gantos recommends reading lots of books, keeping a journal, and writing about what you know. "When I examine my life as a professional writer, I can say without a doubt that starting that first journal was the most important step in my career," he stated. "I hope all of you get journals or diaries and get busy writing about all the interesting things that happen in your lives. Remember, a lot of people think that the 'good stuff' to write about always happens to somebody else. But I believe that the 'good stuff' is always happening to you. Believe this, and you will always have the courage to write something other people want to read."

MARRIAGE AND FAMILY

Jack Gantos married Anne A. Lower, an art dealer, on November 11, 1989. They have one daughter, Mabel Grace, who was born in 1996. The Gantos family lives in Santa Fe, New Mexico.

SELECTED WRITINGS

"Rotten Ralph" Series

Rotten Ralph, 1976
Worse Than Rotten Ralph, 1978
Rotten Ralph's Rotten Christmas, 1984
Rotten Ralph's Trick or Treat, 1986
Rotten Ralph's Show and Tell, 1989
Happy Birthday Rotten Ralph, 1990
Not So Rotten Ralph, 1994
Rotten Ralph Feels Rotten, 1996
Rotten Ralph's Rotten Romance, 1997
The Christmas Spirit Strikes Rotten Ralph, 1998
Rotten Ralph's Halloween Howl, 1998
Back to School for Rotten Ralph, 1998
Rotten Ralph's Thanksgiving Wish, 1999
Wedding Bells for Rotten Ralph, 1999
Rotten Ralph Helps Out, 2001

"Jack Henry" Series

Heads or Tails: Stories from the Sixth Grade, 1994
Jack's New Power: Stories from a Caribbean Year, 1995

Jack's Black Book, 1997
Jack on the Tracks: Four Seasons of Fifth Grade, 1999

"Joey Pigza" Books

Joey Pigza Swallowed the Key, 1998
Joey Pigza Loses Control, 2000

Picture Books

Sleepy Ronald, 1976
Fair-Weather Friends, 1977
Aunt Bernice, 1978
The Perfect Pal, 1979
Greedy Greeny, 1979
Swampy Alligator, 1980
The Werewolf Family, 1980
Willy's Raiders, 1981
Red's Fib, 1985

Other

Zip Six, 1996 (adult novel)
Desire Lines, 1997 (young adult novel)

HONORS AND AWARDS

Emerson Alumni Award (Emerson College): 1979, for outstanding achievement in creative writing
National Endowment for the Arts Grant: 1987
Novella Award (*Quarterly West*): 1989, for "X-Rays"

FURTHER READING

Books

Authors and Artists for Young Adults, Vol. 40
Contemporary Authors New Revision Series, Vol. 97, 2001
Holtze, Sally Holmes, ed. *Fifth Book of Junior Authors and Illustrators,* 1983
Something About the Author, Vol. 119

Periodicals

Albuquerque (NM) Journal, Nov. 15, 1998, p.F4
Allentown (Penn) Morning Call, Sep. 20, 1999, p.D1
Booklist, Mar. 1, 1994, p.1269; Sep. 1, 1999, p.132
Boston Globe, Oct. 2, 1994, p.B18
Boston Herald, Jan. 19, 2001, Arts and Life sec., p.42
Chicago Daily Herald, Nov. 18, 2000, p.D3
Detroit Free Press, July 26, 2001, p.E8
Emergency Librarian, Nov.-Dec. 1997, p.61
Hartford (Conn) Courant, May 8, 2000, p.B1
Horn Book, July-Aug. 1994, p.451; Nov.-Dec. 1996, p.723; Nov. 1998, p.729
New York Times, Nov. 19, 2000, p.L20
Parenting, Apr. 1992, p.30
Santa Fe New Mexican, Jan. 12, 1997, p.E3; Dec. 20, 1998, p.F2
School Library Journal, Sep. 2000, p.228
St. Louis Post-Dispatch, Oct. 10, 1994, p.B1
Teaching Pre K-8, Mar. 1996, p.40
Washington Post, Aug. 14, 2000, p.C13

ADDRESS

Farrar, Straus & Giroux
19 Union Square West
New York, NY 10013

WORLD WIDE WEB SITE

http://www.bookweb.org/news/features/748.html

Aaron McGruder 1974-

American Cartoonist
Creator of "The Boondocks" Comic Strip

BIRTH

Aaron Vincent McGruder was born in May 1974 in Chicago, Illinois. His father, Bill, works as a communications specialist with the National Transportation Safety Board. His mother, Elaine, stayed at home to care for Aaron and his older brother.

YOUTH

When McGruder was a child, his family moved from Chicago to Champaign, Illinois, and then to Louisville, Kentucky. They finally settled in Columbia, Maryland—a suburb of Washington, D.C.—when Aaron was six years old. As one of only a few African-American kids in his neighborhood, McGruder learned about the complexities of race relations at an early age. "I grew up black in middle America," he remembered. "I loved hip-hop, I loved baseball, I loved 'Star Wars' and karate classes—but there [were] alienation and questions of identity, as well."

McGruder enjoyed drawing throughout his childhood. He also loved reading the comics. His favorite strips were "Peanuts" by Charles Schulz and "Bloom County" by Berke Breathed. He liked the depth of emotion in Schulz's work, and the political commentary in Breathed's strip. As a teenager, McGruder often drew comics and tried to come up with ideas for a strip of his own.

EDUCATION

McGruder attended elementary school through high school in Columbia. "Virtually all my life I've been the only black face in class," he related. When he graduated from high school in 1992, he was not sure what career path he wanted to pursue. But he knew that he had a strong interest in art, so he decided to take a year off before starting college and try to get a job as a comic book illustrator. He believed that this career would allow him to combine his interests in art, music, politics, and comic books. He spent his time practicing drawing, attending comic book conventions, and submitting samples of his work to publishers.

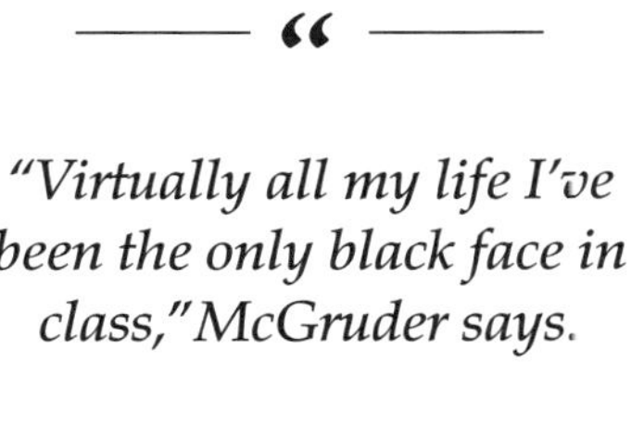

"Virtually all my life I've been the only black face in class," McGruder says.

When he failed to find a job as a comic book illustrator, McGruder enrolled at the University of Maryland. As the final step toward his degree, he wrote a thesis on black cartoonists. As he did research for his paper, he learned that there were only about 10 African-Americans out of over 200 syndicated cartoonists who have their work published in American newspapers. McGruder earned his bachelor's degree in Afro-American Studies in 1997.

CAREER HIGHLIGHTS

Creating His Own Comic Strip

By the time McGruder finished his college degree in 1997, he had already gotten his start as a cartoonist. In 1993, when he was taking a year off from school, he began to notice that the music industry was increasingly marketing hip-hop artists as tough, urban criminals or "gangstas." He did not appreciate seeing African-Americans portrayed in this way. "Everything in hip-hop was street and ghetto and hard," McGruder explained. "I didn't want to be fake. There's always a certain number of black people from the suburbs who really pretend like they're living in the city. It's this notion that you're only truly black if you're from the city and you're poor." He felt that these images reinforced negative stereotypes about blacks. At the same time, he wanted to explore his memories of growing up black in a mostly white suburb. He decided to create a comic strip using satire, which involves making fun of people, political issues, or social movements in order to make a point. McGruder started to develop "The Boondocks," a comic strip that satirized suburban life and hip-hop culture.

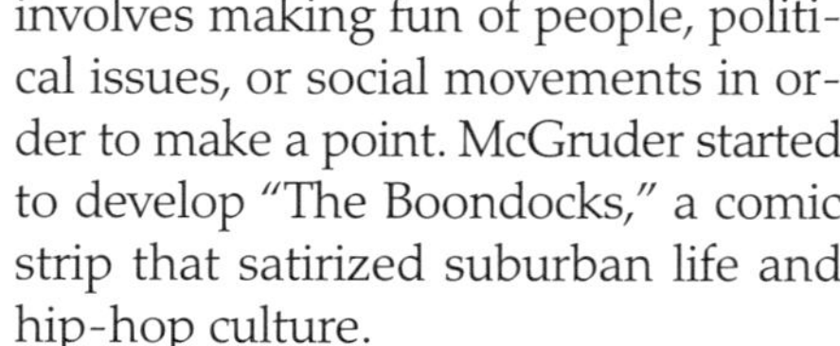

"Everything in hip-hop was street and ghetto and hard. I didn't want to be fake. There's always a certain number of black people from the suburbs who really pretend like they're living in the city. It's this notion that you're only truly black if you're from the city and you're poor."

In February 1996, while he was still in college, McGruder's new comic strip, "The Boondocks," first appeared on a web site called the *Hitlist Online*. In December of that year, his strip began running in the *Diamondback,* the independent student newspaper at the University of Maryland. This early version of "The Boondocks" attracted a great deal of attention, both on campus and across the country. But McGruder pulled his work out of the *Diamondback* two months later, following a disagreement with the editors. In early 1997, the strip appeared briefly in the *Source,* a national hip-hop magazine. Over the years, McGruder sent his strip to several syndication companies—which provide comics to newspapers across the country—but it was rejected.

Shortly after he graduated from college, McGruder attended a convention of the National Association of Black Journalists. While there, he met a representative of Universal Press Syndicate, the company that handles "Peanuts" and many other popular comic strips. She was very impressed with McGruder's comic strip and arranged for her company to syndicate it. In April 1999, "The Boondocks" made its debut in 160 newspapers across the United States. It was an impressive debut, since new comic strips usually launch in only 20 to 30 papers at first.

"The Boondocks"

"The Boondocks" tells the story of two young African-American brothers, Huey and Riley Freeman, who have been transplanted from the urban environment of South Chicago to the fictional, mostly white suburb of Woodcrest. The boys live with their grandfather, who always dreamed of retiring to a nice, quiet neighborhood, far from the problems of the city. As Huey and Riley struggle to adjust to their new surroundings and make new friends there, they make many funny and interesting observations about race relations and life in the "boondocks," as they refer to the suburbs. For example, McGruder jokes about how the boys have to get used to living in a relatively safe area and breathing clean air. He also makes fun of their white neighbors, who react in stereotypical ways: they either become nervous when they see a black face in the neighborhood or expect the boys to be rappers or basketball stars just because of their race. "Featuring four inner-city black kids and a biracial girl trying to get along in the melanin-deprived suburbs, it is a satiric, political comic informed by a hip-hop aesthetic," Lonnae O'Neal Parker wrote after the strip's introduction in the *Washington Post.*

"Huey is the center of the group and who I would be if I knew everything that I know today, what I would be if I was a kid now. When I was in high school, I was somewhat like Huey. I was coming into militancy, learning about the philosophies that Huey embodies."

McGruder describes Huey, the main character of "The Boondocks," as "the eternally scornful champion of the dispossessed." Highly intelligent and deeply opinionated, Huey is on a quest for social justice. He is named after Huey P. Newton, who was a co-founder of the Black Panther Party during the civil rights movement of the 1960s. The Black Panther group was a militant African-American political organization that advocated revolution as the means to black liberation and social equality. Huey Freeman shares many of these revolutionary views. "Huey is the center of the group and who I would be if I knew everything that I know today, what I would be if I was a kid now," McGruder explained. "When I was in high school, I was somewhat like Huey. I was coming into militancy, learning about the philosophies that Huey embodies."

McGruder describes Huey's younger brother, Riley, as "the brash product of a popular black culture obsessed with gangsters." Riley always tries to act tough, like a gangsta. He practices making a mean face, known as a "thug mug," and is disgusted by the fact that strangers consider him cute. He even calls himself "Escobar" after an infamous drug lord. One of Riley's favorite pastimes is trying to frighten his white neighbors. For example, he approaches a well-dressed white man in a red convertible and says, "Nice car." As Riley walks away, he thinks to himself, "Well, that oughta keep HIM awake tonight."

Another character in "The Boondocks" is Jazmine DuBois, a biracial neighbor girl who has trouble deciding whether she is black or white. McGruder noted that Jazmine "personifies identity problems that African-Americans have as a whole. Are we American? Are we African? All of these questions and confusions come into Jazmine." Her friend is Cindy, a white neighbor girl who is excited to meet Huey and Riley because they are black. "So many black people who've grown up in the suburbs have known a girl like Cindy—that one person to whom you are the most fascinating curiosity," McGruder stated. "They want to touch your hair and ask you all kinds of inane questions about rap music. You're this thing that was previously only on their television screen and now you're there in real life."

McGruder draws "The Boondocks" in a distinctive style that is influenced by Japanese animation, or anime. The characters have high foreheads, big, expressive eyes, and small, sharp facial features. McGruder draws the comic by hand, then does all the lettering, shading, and coloring on a computer. In a review of early strips for the *Onion,* Keith Phipps said that "The Boondocks" had "the right combination of winning characters, effective gags, and storylines that didn't shy away from racial issues and other political material."

Race and Satire

McGruder has often talked about the background of his creation. He said that the comic strip "shouldn't be taken as autobiographical. But I think all of the characters come from me. They represent larger issues and larger facets of the black community." McGruder based the humor on his own experiences growing up in the suburbs, as well as his study of African-American history. "The strip is meant to be an intelligent and satirical view of black/white relationships as well as black/black relationships," he noted. "This is simply because I have a lifetime of experience in these areas—and to effectively and intelligently poke fun at something as potentially explosive as race relations requires an in-depth knowledge of subtleties and nuances of the racial dynamic—not to mention an awareness of the line between humor and offense."

According to McGruder, "The Boondocks" is intended to reflect the unique experiences and viewpoints of himself and his African-American readers. "It's unapologetically a black strip, a hip-hop strip in its urban sensibility and language and the perspective of its characters. Hip-hop shaped my world view to a great extent, not in its commercial, mainstream sense but more in terms of being an expression of the collective experience of black people," he explained. "I'm a black artist, and this is a reflection of me. I feel I have a responsibility to the black community, to represent us accurately and depict us in both writing and art in a way in which black people will be proud and allow their children to read it."

McGruder has often talked about the background of his creation. He has said that the comic strip "shouldn't be taken as autobiographical. But I think all of the characters come from me. They represent larger issues and larger facets of the black community."

But McGruder argues that the issue of race is only one part of the strip; he also claims that the relationships among the characters are key to the success of the strip. "People focus on the sensationalism of the race issues, but they don't discuss the humanity of the characters," he says. That view was echoed by Stephanie Kang in *Los Angeles Magazine,* where she wrote, "In the end, it's the characters that give 'The Boondocks' its authenticity, whether detailing the conflicts of navigating a black identity in a white world or dealing with universal issues of family and school. Just as Lucy never lets Charlie Brown kick that football, Huey will continue procrastinating about mowing the lawn, and Riley will always, always whup Huey on PlayStation 2. These everyday moments are as integral a part of 'The Boondocks' freshness as its social commentary."

Popular But Controversial

When "The Boondocks" made its 1999 debut in newspapers across the country, the response from readers was overwhelming—both positive and negative. In fact, McGruder's work generated more discussion during its first few months of publication than most comic strips do in decades. Some people loved "The Boondocks" and considered it a brilliant and sly social satire. But many other people hated the comic strip and called it mean-spirited, degrading, and racist. Because of the controversy, McGruder ended up appearing on television news programs and being inter-

viewed by magazines and newspapers across the country, which brought the strip even more attention.

Some critics have claimed that McGruder intentionally tries to provoke people with his comic strip. They use words like "edge" and "attitude" to describe his work, and argue that he is more concerned with stirring up controversy than with creating humor. In fact, several newspapers run "The Boondocks" not in the comics section but instead in the editorial section, where writers present their social and political views. But McGruder says that his emphasis is always on humor. "It's not written to be edgy for its own sake. It's written to be funny. But any time you're speaking about race, you're labeled as having an 'edge.' And young black males are often said to have an 'attitude,'" he noted. "What I don't want is for controversy to be the gimmick of the strip. That would play itself out pretty quick."

Other people have objected to the ways in which McGruder discusses racial issues. But he feels that it is important to discuss race openly. "Some people think it's racist to even discuss race," he once said. "A strip like mine is bound to make some people mad." Some critics argue that, rather than promoting understanding between the races, McGruder is insulting both white people and black people and increasing the racial divisions in American society. Yet others would say that he is challenging and enlightening both racial groups. "People are amazed that I say the things I say to mainstream America. But it really shouldn't be that big a deal. The problem is that information is so controlled and limited in this country that other perspectives are quickly seen as offensive or subversive," he stated. "It was such a big deal when it first came out that these racial issues were being discussed so frankly, and I think in a very short amount of time people realized that the world didn't end and the strip's still there."

———— " ————

"['The Boondocks' is] unapologetically a black strip, a hip-hop strip in its urban sensibility and language and the perspective of its characters. Hip-hop shaped my world view to a great extent, not in its commercial, mainstream sense but more in terms of being an expression of the collective experience of black people. I'm a black artist, and this is a reflection of me. I feel I have a responsibility to the black community, to represent us accurately and depict us in both writing and art in a way in which black people will be proud and allow their children to read it."

Some critics have called "The Boondocks" mean-spirited, especially when McGruder makes personal attacks on such people as presidential candidates George W. Bush and Al Gore, the Reverend Jesse Jackson, and rap artist Sean "Puffy" Combs. One particular target has been Robert L. Johnson, the president of BET (Black Entertainment Television), whom McGruder has repeatedly lambasted for what he views as the exploitive and degrading programming on BET.

Others critics have argued that "The Boondocks" promotes violence to children. In one controversial installment, Riley hits Cindy over the head with a plastic *Star Wars* light saber, then becomes upset when she is not hurt. Many have expressed disappointment that this violent episode would appear in the comics. Yet others have pointed to such revered strips as "Peanuts," where Lucy often smacks other characters, as evidence that such violence wasn't new to the funny pages. In another controversial episode, Huey appears to threaten a teacher by saying "the day of reckoning fast approaches." That particularly angered people because it ran just after an incident in which a teacher was killed by a student in a Florida school. But comic strips are completed weeks in advance of their publication, so McGruder clearly was not responding to the tragedy. Some viewed this as further evidence of the double standard in criticism of his work.

BOONDOCKS © Aaron McGruder. Dist. by UNIVERSAL PRESS SYNDICATE. Preprinted with permission. All rights reserved.

McGruder responds to such criticism by emphasizing that "The Boondocks" is a work of satire, which can make some people uncomfortable. He says that those who do not like the strip simply should not read it. "What the strip is ultimately about is who we are as black people, what it means to be black, and black self-identity. It's a racial satire. A social satire. Sometimes a political satire," McGruder noted. "I'm trying to give young black children out there something I didn't have growing up. Something that wasn't corny or contrived. . . . One of the things I've tried to do was. . . show the sophistication and the intelligence of young black kids today."

McGruder's controversial approach to contemporary topics caused a handful of newspapers to drop "The Boondocks" since its debut. At the same time, however, many other papers picked up the strip. In fact, distribution of the comic strip expanded to nearly 300 newspapers around the country by mid-2001.

Recent Activities

In addition to his ongoing comic strip, McGruder has published two books of collected cartoons: *The Boondocks: Because I Know You Don't Read the Newspaper* (2000) and *Fresh for '01 . . . You Suckas* (2001). He has also started adapting "The Boondocks" as an animated television series. For that project he's working with Reginald Hudlin, the director of the films *House Party*, *Boomerang*, and *The Ladies Man*.

Recently, McGruder was one of the first cartoonists to begin to deal with the issues related to the September 11 terrorist attacks on the World Trade Center in New York City and the Pentagon in Washington, D.C. It's a risky topic for satire, since the incidents are still so recent and so devastating. But McGruder didn't want to shy away from this difficult topic: "I ultimately made the decision to deal with it because I feel that's why I got in cartooning in the first place, to address these issues. For me, the way the media was covering [the attacks] and the way the politicians were acting seemed fair enough game. . . . I think if there's an incident that's worth ruining your career over, this is it. I'm always afraid I'll regret not having said something, small as my voice may be." In fact, McGruder feels strongly that he has a responsibility to speak out. "I feel America started moving very quickly in a dangerous direction with this drumbeating and warmongering. 'They're evil and we're not' is such a [childish] way of looking at conflict. It is the responsibility of any thinking individual with a voice to say whatever they can within their medium. You can't underestimate the power of one voice."

"

"What the strip is ultimately about is who we are as black people, what it means to be black, and black self-identity. It's a racial satire. A social satire. Sometimes a political satire. I'm trying to give young black children out there something I didn't have growing up. Something that wasn't corny or contrived. . . . One of the things I've tried to do was . . . show the sophistication and the intelligence of young black kids today."

ADVICE TO ASPIRING CARTOONISTS

McGruder offers this advice to aspiring cartoonists: "Hire a lawyer. You can lose everything that you create by signing away your rights and not even know it. Work on your writing and drawing. When it comes to submitting your ideas and what editors choose, you can't control that. But you can control the quality of what you are putting out."

MAJOR INFLUENCES

McGruder gives credit to several cartoonists who have influenced his work, particularly Charles Schulz. McGruder recalls here that he began reading "Peanuts" when he was young. He soon moved on to other cartoons, but "Peanuts" had a lasting impression on him over the years. "Oh I read it, just not very often, and not since I was very young. By the fourth grade I had moved on to 'Garfield' [Jim Davis], and several years later, to the strip that would ultimately make me want to do this for a living, 'Bloom County' {Berke Breathed]. Shortly thereafter, I discovered the genius of Bill Watterson ['Calvin and Hobbes'] and Garry Trudeau ['Doonesbury']. . . . [To] put it in some perspective—if Breathed taught me how to be a cartoonist, Schulz taught me how to be a human being. If Watterson taught me how to tell a joke, Schulz taught me which jokes to tell. 'Peanuts' has always been so much more than a comic strip. These were my first life lessons. Be down with the underdog, empathize with the victimized, life isn't always fair, Christmas is too commercial, most of your friends will laugh at you at the earliest opportunity, girls will pull away at the last second and leave you screaming flat on your back (hey, one did it to me just this summer), and above all, KEEP YOUR HEAD UP."

(For more information on these cartoonists, see Schulz in *Biography Today Author Series,* Vol. 2, and Update in 2000 Cumulation; see Davis in *Biography Today Author Series,* Vol. 1; see Breathed in *Biography Today,* Jan. 1992; see Watterson in *Biography Today,* Jan. 1992.)

HOME AND FAMILY

When McGruder first syndicated his cartoon to newspapers he was still living in his old bedroom at his parents' house. Currently, he lives in a one-bedroom apartment in the Los Feliz neighborhood of Los Angeles, California. He is single.

HOBBIES AND OTHER INTERESTS

McGruder claims that he is too busy to have much time for a social life. He says that he has "no BMW, no Benz, not a single article of clothing from Versace or FUBU, and no life as a result." McGruder also admits that he has very little interest in today's popular culture. "I don't watch television. I go to very few movies," he stated. "The comic strips I read . . . I generally just go back and read 'Calvin and Hobbes' or something that's already been out. There are very few places to go. Even music sucks. The only CDs I'm buying are old CDs, and the only music I'm listening to is stuff that was out five to ten years ago." Although he was disappointed in *The Phantom Menace,* McGruder still considers himself a fan of *Star Wars* and has a large collection of *Star Wars* toys. He also admits that he is addicted to eating dry Life cereal.

WRITINGS

The Boondocks: Because I Know You Don't Read the Newspaper, 2000
Fresh for '01 . . . You Suckas, 2001

FURTHER READING

Periodicals

Atlanta Constitution, June 2, 1999, p.C1
Baltimore Sun, Apr. 19, 1999, p.E1; July 5, 1999, p.E1
Black Enterprise, July 2000, p.64
Dallas Morning News, Apr. 15, 1999, p.C1
Denver Post, Sep. 5, 1999, p.H1
Detroit News, Apr. 17, 1999, p.C1
Guardian (London), Feb. 14, 2000, Media sec., p.2
Los Angeles Magazine, Aug. 1, 2001, p.60
Los Angeles Times, June 9, 1999, p.E1
Minneapolis Star-Tribune, Apr. 19, 1999, p.E1; June 6, 1999, p.F1; Nov. 8, 1999, p.E1
New York Times Magazine, June 24, 2001, p.42

Newsday, Aug. 5, 1999, p.B3
Newsweek, July 5, 1999, p.59
People, July 26, 1999, p.125
Seattle Post-Intelligencer, June 28, 1999, p.C1
Time, July 5, 1999, p.78
Washington Post, Aug. 20, 1997, p.C1; Apr. 26, 1999, p.C1; June 20, 1999, p.B6; Nov. 22, 1999, p.C1

Other

Biography Resource Center Online, 2000

ADDRESS

Universal Press Syndicate
4520 Main Street
Kansas City, MO 64111

WORLD WIDE WEB SITES

http://www.boondocks.net
http://www.ucomics.com

Richard Peck 1934-

American Novelist for Young Adults
Author of *A Year Down Yonder*, Winner of the 2001 Newbery Medal

BIRTH

Richard Wayne Peck was born April 5, 1934, in Decatur, Illinois. His mother, Virginia Gray, was trained as a dietician. His father, Wayne Peck, owned a Phillips 66 gas station in Decatur. He has one younger sister, Cheryl.

YOUTH

Peck spent his childhood surrounded by a large and loving family that included grandparents, aunts, uncles, and assorted other relations. A number of these relatives were very colorful characters, including his Uncle Miles (who seemed to know gossip about everyone in Decatur) and his own father (a World War I veteran who loved to ride his Harley Davidson motorcycle around town). In fact, Peck has stated that the personalities and lifestyles of many of his relatives eventually became models for characters in his young adult novels. "When you write for young readers, you need the wisdom of those people at the other end of life," he explained. "I came to writing with an entire crew of seasoned elders on my side."

Peck attributes his life-long love for books to his mother, who encouraged him to read and write from an early age. "I came from a home where no [television] screens glowed, a home where there were bedtime stories because there was bedtime," he later explained. "My mother read to me before I could read for myself. She had no intention of sending an ignoramus to first grade, and so she filled me up with words and opened the door to the alternative universe of storytelling, of fiction. I heard my first stories in my mother's voice."

"I came from a home where no [television] screens glowed, a home where there were bedtime stories because there was bedtime. My mother read to me before I could read for myself. She had no intention of sending an ignoramus to first grade, and so she filled me up with words and opened the door to the alternative universe of storytelling, of fiction. I heard my first stories in my mother's voice."

During Peck's teen years in Decatur, the city's small-town atmosphere comforted him, but also made him restless. He felt safe and secure in his hometown, where he was nestled among family and friends. But literature and films showed him that an exciting world lay beyond Decatur's city limits, and he became impatient to experience some of that world first-hand.

Early in 1950 Peck received an unexpected offer from a relative living in New York City. The relative invited the 16-year-old boy to spend part of his upcoming summer in the city, provided he earned the necessary traveling money himself. The offer delighted Peck, who spent the next several months shoveling snow and raking leaves around the neighborhood to earn money for his train ticket. When he finally arrived in New York, he discovered that he loved the hustle and bustle of the big city. "It came as quite a relief to me that the outside world was really there and somewhat better than the movies," he said. "I began to explore the streets of New York and plumb the depths of the subway system all the way to Coney Island [a tourist attraction on the far outskirts of the city]. It occurred to me that this was the place I'd been homesick for all along, this place and London."

"

Peck has said that he might never have developed into a talented writer without the instruction of a stern high school English teacher named Miss Franklin. "She knew the danger of inspiration coming before grammar. She knew that without the framework for sharing, ideas are nothing. I [did not] write a line of fiction until I was 37 years old, but it was Miss F. who made it possible. In the boot camp atmosphere of her classroom she taught us that the only real writing is rewriting. She taught us that deadlines are meant to be met, not extended. She taught us how to gather material more interesting than ourselves and to pin it on a page."

"

EDUCATION

Peck was a good and obedient student who ranked among the top students at both Woodrow Wilson Junior High School and Stephen Decatur High School. Peck later credited his fine academic performance to a deep fear of missing out on college. "I did homework out of fear, not good," he admitted. "From junior high on, I thought that the only safe way to a scholarship was a string of A's on the report card." Peck took his other youthful responsibilities—such as an after-school paper route—seriously as well. He recognized that the adult world around him respected reliability and hard work, and he was determined to gain acceptance into that world as soon as possible.

In the meantime, Peck's passion for literature continued to grow. He loved reading about all sorts of subjects, and enjoyed writing short stories and other compositions. But years after completing high school, he said that he might never have developed into a talented writer without the instruction of a stern English teacher named Miss Franklin. "She knew the danger of inspiration coming before grammar," he recalled. "She knew that without the framework for sharing, ideas are nothing. I [did not] write a line of fiction until I was 37 years old, but it was Miss F. who made it possible. In the boot camp atmosphere of her classroom she taught us that the only real writing is rewriting. She taught us that deadlines are meant to be met, not extended. She taught us how to gather material more interesting than ourselves and to pin it on a page." Peck graduated from Stephen Decatur High School in 1952.

College Years

Peck enrolled at DePauw University in Greencastle, Indiana, where he decided to pursue a teaching degree. He later recalled that the threat of the Korean War hung over himself and his fellow students throughout his first few semesters at DePauw. This conflict between the Asian nations of South and North Korea raged from 1950 to 1953. It eventually drew 19 countries into the fighting, including the United States, and resulted in over 140,000 casualties (killed, wounded, and missing soldiers). Peck recalled that many of the American soldiers who served in the war were not volunteers, but draftees who were legally required to join the military (during this period in American history, the government maintained a military "draft" to fill the ranks of its armed services). "If a boy didn't maintain a college grade point average in the upper half of his class, the university informed his local draft board, and he soon found himself in Korea," remembered Peck. "When I was a freshman, one of the seniors in the fraternity allowed his grades to slip and was drafted out of the school in mid-semester. This had an electrifying effect on the rest of us, and we all became a lot more scholarly than we'd meant to be. Silent study hours were invoked and homework seminars were set up in the dining room. It was far from an animal-house environment."

The highlight of Peck's undergraduate years was 1954, when he spent his entire junior year at Exeter University in England. Peck recalled his year in Europe as one of the most stimulating and fascinating of his life. He en-

joyed studying literature and British history under Exeter's instructors, and he spent much of his free time roaming the cities of Europe by train and boat. He reluctantly returned to DePauw at the end of his junior year and graduated in 1956.

Peck entered the U.S. Army within weeks of his graduation, and he spent the next two years stationed in Europe. Peck's service in the U.S. Army began three years after the end of the Korean War, and to his surprise he actually enjoyed his military experience. He spent two years stationed in Germany, where he worked as a company clerk and chaplain's assistant. He even worked as a "ghostwriter" of sermons for several chaplains at the military base. A ghostwriter is someone who writes something that is actually credited to another person. Peck later claimed that his sermon-writing gave him valuable experience in developing composition skills and meeting writing deadlines.

Peck's military service also gave him the opportunity to resume his exploration of Europe. Peck spent many of his off-duty hours exploring the cities of Germany, and he used his leaves (military vacations) to venture into neighboring European countries, just as he had done during his school days. But although he enjoyed many aspects of his tour, he was still happy to leave army life behind in 1958, when his military obligation ended. He promptly returned to America, where he enrolled in graduate school at Southern Illinois University at Carbondale. One year later, armed with a master's degree in English, he became an instructor at Southern Illinois.

CAREER HIGHLIGHTS

In the four decades since Peck graduated from Southern Illinois University, he has become one of America's most popular and respected authors of novels for young adults. He has written more than two dozen works targeted at young people, using fiction to explore themes of friendship, loneliness, peer pressure, self-respect, and other topics of interest to teens. Many of Peck's novels also deal with important issues that confront many adolescents, such as divorce, teen pregnancy, suicide, rape, and the death of loved ones. But readers and critics alike agree that Peck is able to write about these topics in an interesting and entertaining way, employing humor, supernatural elements, and dramatic plot twists. As Hilary Crew wrote in *Top of the News,* "[Peck's] variety of characters and his use of history can extend the horizons of an adolescent. Add a dash of the supernatural, a great sense of humor, and a real interest in and understanding of the problems of adolescents, and you have a successful writer for young adults."

Starting Out as a Teacher

Peck's first professional career was teaching. He remained on the campus at Southern Illinois University after receiving his master's degree in English, joining the faculty of the school. He spent two years teaching English at the university before accepting a teaching position at Glenbrook North High School in Northbrook, Illinois.

When Peck arrived in the wealthy suburb of Northbrook in 1961, the attitudes of the majority of the student body stunned and angered him. He felt that most of the teens he encountered were self-centered and unmotivated, with little interest in improving themselves. These feelings did not stop him from preparing inventive and challenging lesson plans, but they triggered Peck's first doubts about staying with a teaching career.

"[As] a teacher, I'd already learned that you can only teach those who are willing to be taught. I'd learned too, that the best, most independent, most promising students were the thoughtful, quiet ones — students who will reach for a book in search of themselves — who often get overlooked in our crisis-oriented society and the schools that mirror it."

In 1963 Peck briefly left the teaching profession to work as a textbook editor for publisher Scott, Foresman and Company in Chicago. During his time there he wrote his first book, a guide to Chicago nightlife called *Old Town, A Complete Guide: Strolling, Shopping, Supping, and Sipping* (1965). But less than two years after his arrival in Chicago, he accepted a teaching position at Hunter College and Hunter College High School in New York City, where he had long dreamed of living.

Peck loved living and working in the heart of America's largest city. But his frustration with teaching grew at Hunter College High School, a school for academically gifted girls. He felt that many of his students were spoiled and lazy, in part because of a lack of parental guidance and encouragement. He also felt that the school administration did not challenge students to perform to the best of their abilities. Despite his growing unhappiness, Peck continued to work hard to spark his students' interest in literature and current events. But as time passed, he admitted that "it seemed to me that teaching had begun to turn into something that looked weirdly like psychiatric social work — a field in which I was not trained or interested."

As Peck's disillusionment with teaching increased, he began thinking about a writing career. His interest in switching careers was further heightened when he co-edited several collections of essays and poems, including *Edge of Awareness* (1966) and *Sounds and Silences: Poetry for Now* (1970). His work on these projects also gave him an opportunity to meet a number of respected agents and editors in New York's publishing industry.

Becoming a Writer

In 1971 Peck finally resigned from his teaching position to devote his energies to becoming a novelist. This decision was risky, for he was leaving behind the security of a steady job that provided him with a comfortable salary, medical insurance, and a retirement plan. But he later said that he was determined to succeed as a writer. "I didn't even worry about what I was going to do to make a living if [writing] didn't work," he stated.

But although Peck decided to leave the classroom, he did not give up on teaching teenagers. In fact, he felt that with his firsthand knowledge of the attitudes and behaviors of adolescents, he could use writing as a tool to pass along some important lessons about life. In addition, he felt that some students might be particularly open to the sort of stories he wanted to write. He decided to aim directly at "students who were willing and able to spend a part of their time with books" because "as a teacher, I'd already learned that you can only teach those who are willing to be taught. I'd learned too, that the best, most independent, most promising students were the thoughtful, quiet ones — students who will reach for a book in search of themselves — who often get overlooked in our crisis-oriented society and the schools that mirror it."

Peck's first novel for young adults was *Don't Look and It Won't Hurt*, published in 1972. Many critics praised the work, which tackled the sensitive subject of teen pregnancy. The *New York Times Book Review,* for example, stated that "Mr. Peck's is a textured story of three daughters in a desperately poor home headed by a mother who is both defeated and proud. Through the insightful eyes of the middle child we come to understand the complex forces that lead to the eldest girl's pregnancy. . . . Rather than arousing judgmental passions, *Don't Look and It Won't Hurt* leaves the reader . . . terribly moved." (Twenty years after it was first published, this novel was turned into the 1992 movie *Gas, Food, Lodging,* but Peck hated the film because its creators added graphic language and changed many of the events in his book.)

In 1973 Peck published *Dreamland Lake,* a YA (young adult) mystery novel about a 13-year-old boy whose summer takes a dark turn when he and a friend discover the body of an old tramp deep in the woods. This novel also received good reviews. "Beautifully told, the story has just enough foreshadowing to heighten the sense of impending doom," commented *School Library Journal.*

Two years later, Peck introduced one of his best-known fictional characters in *The Ghost Belonged to Me,* an entertaining tale of the supernatural. The action in this novel centers around Blossom Culp, a spunky girl with psychic powers who is able to communicate with ghosts. Blossom lives in the early 20th century in a small Illinois town patterned after Peck's own hometown of Decatur. But in both *The Ghost Belonged to Me* and three other books about Blossom—*Ghosts I Have Been* (1977), *The Dreadful Future of Blossom Culp* (1983), and *Sleep of Death* (1986)—she and her friend Alexander journey around the world and through time to investigate ghostly happenings.

Growing Reputation as a YA Novelist

In 1976 Peck released *Are You in the House Alone,* which remains one of his best-known books. The novel focuses on the emotional struggles of a teenage girl after she is raped by the son of one of her community's most powerful families. Peck wrote the book in part because he wanted to bring attention to a problem—teen vulnerability to rape and other forms of sexual abuse—that many people were reluctant to talk about. But he also stated that the book is "*not* a single-problem novel. It's about the consequences of being a young victim, regardless of the crime, a young victim in a society filling up with them. In an age of daily papers and late news bulletins, we

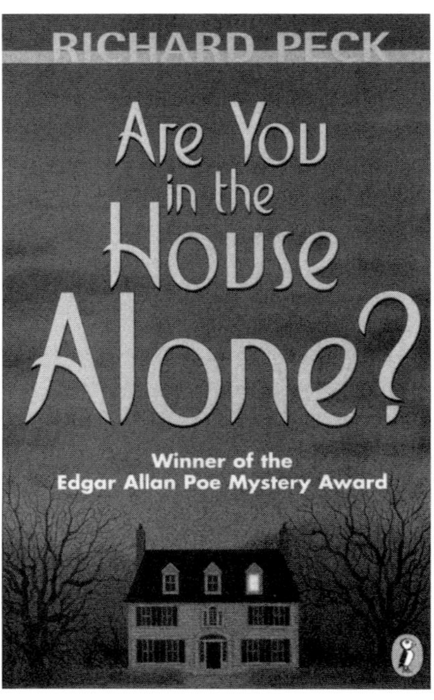

rarely learn how life does and does not go on for former victims."

Are You in the House Alone? earned many awards and received significant critical attention. Zena Sutherland, writing in *Bulletin of the Center for Children's Books,* wrote that "It isn't *what* happens that gives the story impact, although that is handled with conviction, and although the style, dialogue, and characters are equally impressive —it is the honest and perceptive way that the author treats the problem of rape. For Peck sees clearly both society's problem and the victim's: the range of attitudes, the awful indignity, the ramifications of fear and shame." A reviewer in the *New York Times Book Review* thought that portions of the book were too melodramatic. But the critic also admitted that her 15-year-old daughter was tremendously moved by the book. In 1978 a film adaptation of the novel starring Kathleen Beller, Dennis Quaid, and Blythe Danner appeared on network television.

Peck's next book was *Father Figure* (1978), which the author still regards as one of his best YA novels. The plot centers around Jim, a 17-year-old boy who cares for his 8-year-old brother after their mother dies. The novel traces his thoughts and emotions when he and his brother are forced to go live with their father, who had abandoned them several years earlier. "Peck's new novel [is] the best of many that have won him honors, and assuredly one of the best for all ages in many a moon," commented *Publishers Weekly.* "Peck makes everyone so human and interesting that readers believe in and care about one and all." In 1980 *Father Figure* was made into a television movie starring Hal Linden and Timothy Hutton.

Writing Both to Entertain and to Inspire

By the early 1980s, Peck was firmly established as one of America's leading novelists for young adults. But he recognized that if he did not make a special effort to talk with teenagers about their fears, hopes, and experiences, his writing would eventually suffer. "At your typewriter you're aging every minute while, mysteriously, your readers remain the same age," he explained. "Worse yet, they change their protective coloring, their fads in clothes and speech and music, every semester." With this in mind, Peck established a travel routine that takes him to dozens of schools and libraries every year. In fact, he travels an estimated 50,000 to 70,000 miles annually in order to visit with teen audiences.

Peck's busy schedule helps him to learn about the concerns of each new generation of middle- and high-school students. But he believes that the underlying message of his writing remains the same from novel to novel. "A young adult novel is the chronicle of one step in a young character's climb to maturity. It can be comic, tragic, and often faltering, but it is always a step up," he said. His books also emphasize that maturity can not be reached without gaining self-respect and independence from peer pressure. In fact, Peck claims that the message he returns to again and again in his YA novels is that "You will never begin to grow up until you start to act and think independently of your peers."

———— " ————

Peck has this advice for his readers: "You will never begin to grow up until you start to act and think independently of your peers."

———— " ————

Peck recognizes, however, that even the most worthwhile message will be ignored if it comes in a dull and boring package. With this in mind, he admits that "in most of my novels, morals and themes lurk beneath the window-dressing of suspense or humor or local color or wish-fulfillment or melodrama or escapism or fantasy or the supernatural." But he adds that teaching kids to enjoy reading of any kind is a significant reward all by itself: "The young will live in as small a world as they can unless they get a nudging from the nest and . . . if they do not start early to read about a wider world, they will never be a part of it. . . . My goal in life is to keep young people reading—I've given my life to it."

Continued Success in the 1980s and 1990s

Peck remained one of the nation's most respected YA novelists throughout the 1980s and 1990s. He occasionally tried his hand at adult novels during this time. In 1980, for instance, he published *Amanda/Miranda,* a well-received historical novel about a selfish, wealthy young woman (Amanda) and her innocent servant (Miranda). It's an enthralling adventure story

about what happens during a fateful impersonation attempt on board the Titanic. Although Peck wrote the novel for adults, it was so popular with teen readers that he later revised it in 1999 in a special abridged version for young adults.

Despite his writings for adults, Peck's continued interest in teens has always led him back to issues and plots of interest to adolescents. During the 1980s, for instance, he penned several books that hit home with YA audiences. In the 1981 book *Close Enough to Touch,* the author wrote about a boy's grief after his girlfriend's sudden death. The book did not receive universal praise. *School Library Journal,* for instance, complained that the plot and characters were predictable. But other reviewers hailed Peck for writing a book about emotional loss from the perspective of a male teen, and *Publishers Weekly* stated that the novel displayed Peck's "grace and wit and—most of all—understanding of confused teenagers."

Another highly regarded Peck book of the 1980s was *Princess Ashley* (1987), a YA novel about a girl who spends so much time worrying about her peers' opinions that she fails to develop her own personality and identity. This book also proved popular with critics and teens alike. Peck "deftly captures the evolving concerns of 15- and 16-year-olds—their speech, anxieties, and shifting relationships with parents and peers," wrote *Kirkus Reviews.* A reviewer for *School Library Journal* wrote that "the characters, both adult and adolescent, are expertly drawn and totally believable. Peck obviously knows how teenagers think and feel, and this insight enables him to bring his characters vibrantly to life." A year later, Peck published *Those Summer Girls I Never Met* (1988), in which two children learn to respect and love their grandmother after they are forced to accompany her on a cruise.

Peck continued to explore new subjects and genres in the 1990s. In 1995, for instance, he published *The Last Safe Place on Earth,* a serious YA novel that condemned book censorship. Yet during the same period, Peck wrote two lighthearted books that blended humor, science-fiction, and time travel—*Lost in Cyberspace* (1995) and *The Great Interactive Dream Machine* (1996). Then, in 1998, Peck unveiled *Strays Like Us,* a powerful story about two young people who forge a special friendship when family relationships crumble around them. "Peck is at his best in this wry, unsentimental story of three generations in small-town Missouri: their roots, their failures, their loving kindness," commented *Booklist.*

A Long Way from Chicago

Peck is grateful that his YA novels have received numerous honors and awards over the years. But he recently published two books that have received special recognition. In 1999, Peck published his novel *A Long Way from Chicago.* This story is set during the 1930s, when the "Great Depression"—a period of terrible economic hardship and poverty—shook American communities from coast to coast. *A Long Way from Chicago* is told from the perspective of a teenage boy named Joey. He and his little sister Mary Alice live in Chicago, but they are sent to spend the summer with their Grandma Dowdel out in the Illinois countryside. Once they arrive, they discover that their grandmother is a proud and adventurous soul who launches all sorts of schemes to help the poor people in her small town. The books consists of eight chapters or stories told by Joey, one each for the seven summers that he and Mary Alice spend with their grandmother, plus one story that Joey tells after he passes through town several years later. Grandma Dowdel provides the moral focus of the story, and Peck earned praise for this portrayal of a strong, older character who teaches the children life lessons. "The young are more desperate than ever for strong leadership, which Grandma Dowdel clearly represents," Peck says. "In 1937, adults still ruled the world." Others also found the character of Grandma Dowdel particularly riveting. "Grandma Dowdel is a force of nature, and try as you might to outsmart her or second guess her, you can't. That's very appealing in that it adds an element of mystery," said Caroline Parr, librarian and chair of the Newbery Award Selection Committee.

A Long Way from Chicago was very well received by reviewers and readers. These tall tales skillfully capture the voices and attitudes of small-town Depression-era life, critics noted, with stories that range from poignant to humorous to eccentric to outrageous. "Each tale is a small masterpiece of storytelling," one reviewer wrote in *Horn Book*, "and taken as a whole, the novel reveals a strong sense of place, a depth of characterization, and a rich sense of humor." *A Long Way from Chicago* was named an ALA Best Book for Young Adults, a Newbery Honor book, and a finalist for the National Book Award, some of the greatest honors that any book can receive.

Peck still feels a deep need to communicate with teenagers. "I think what they are looking for is emotional content. I think what they want is warmth and belonging, which is so hard to find in a suburb. In a suburb, a child sees money spent but not money earned. That's a very skewed view of the world."

A Year Down Yonder

One year later, Peck published a sequel to *A Long Way from Chicago* called *A Year Down Yonder*. In this work, 15-year-old Mary Alice is returned to her grandmother's care when her parents are unable to feed and clothe her. Peck then spins an entertaining, witty story of love and friendship across generations. While *A Long Way from Chicago* focused on Grandma, *A Year Down Yonder* also focuses on Mary Alice, as she grows up, finds a role model in an unexpected place, and develops a new respect and affection for her iconoclastic grandmother. "[Grandma's] escapades will once again make readers laugh," observed a review in *Book*. "Yet she is also so hard-working, imaginative, and loyal that, in the end, Mary Alice finds it surprisingly hard to leave, just as readers will be sorry to close the book after its poignant final chapter."

A Year Down Yonder appealed to critics and readers alike. In fact, Peck's book was so well-written that it received the 2001 Newbery Medal, the highest award in children's literature. In announcing the award, Caroline Parr, chair of the Newbery Award Selection Committee, said this: "Peck's characters are fully realized, from the quiet widow nursing her war-injured son, to Maxine Patch, running out of Grandma's house draped only in the biggest snake outside the Brookfield Zoo," she said. "These stories will, like Maxine, streak 'straight into the annals of undying fame.'" Parr is a big fan of Peck's

novel: "It's a very entertaining book. It's skillfully done. He knows how to tell a story. There's an amazing amount of character development" for such a short book, she says. "There's no word or sentence that's not necessary."

Peck was thrilled to win the Newbery Medal. But he did not take long to savor the honor before returning to work. In late 2001 he published *Fair Weather,* another historical novel for young adults. *Fair Weather* follows the adventures of Rosie, a teenage girl from a small farm town, when she and her family attend the 1893 World's Fair in Chicago. It also features an older character, Granddad, who Peck says is an homage to the writer Mark Twain and also to his great-uncle. The book was inspired, he once wrote, by his own childhood wish to attend a World's Fair: "Possibly because I didn't get to go to a World's Fair in my childhood, I've wanted to go ever since, even if I have to write the book to get there."

Current Thoughts

Even after three decades of writing, Peck still feels a deep need to communicate with teenagers. "I think what they are looking for is emotional content," he said. "I think what they want is warmth and belonging, which is so hard to find in a suburb. In a suburb, a child sees money spent but not money earned. That's a very skewed view of the world." He also believes that the middle school years are the most difficult years of many people's lives. "I get letters every day, very sad letters [from middle school children]," stated Peck. "Their letters reek of loneliness." He hopes that his YA novels carry a message to these and other lonely and misunderstood teens that they are not alone, and that their future lives can be rich and rewarding.

Peck is deeply concerned about the horrific events of September 11, when terrorists attacked the World Trade Center and the Pentagon. Like everyone, he reacted with sorrow and anger. But he is also deeply worried about how these events will affect his teen readers. "It stirs another thing in me — how unaware our teen-age children are of the world, how little they know of the geography and politics of the world. The only thing they know about is their peer group. They have the vulnerability of refusing to know about the world, and we, as adults, have given up trying to tell them." In light of these attacks, Peck feels a special urgency to write historical fiction that can illuminate the past for young readers. "History isn't a folded-up map," he says. "Now we know history is a fireman's child, waiting alone."

"

In light of the terrorist attacks on September 11, Peck feels a special urgency to write historical fiction that can illuminate the past for young readers. "History isn't a folded-up map," he says. "Now we know history is a fireman's child, waiting alone."

"

HOME AND FAMILY

Peck has never been married, and he has no children. He has lived in the Manhattan area of New York City for the past three decades.

HOBBIES AND OTHER INTERESTS

Peck enjoys reading books about different historical events and eras. He also occasionally serves as an instructor of creative writing on cruise ships traveling to and from Europe.

SELECTED WRITINGS

Novels for Young Adults

Don't Look and It Won't Hurt, 1972
Dreamland Lake, 1973
Through a Brief Darkness, 1973
Representing Superdoll, 1974
The Ghost Belonged to Me, 1975
Are You in the House Alone? 1976
Ghosts I Have Seen, 1977
Father Figure, 1978
Secrets of the Shopping Mall, 1979
Close Enough to Touch, 1981
The Dreadful Future of Blossom Culp, 1983
Remembering the Good Times, 1985
Blossom Culp and the Sleep of Death, 1986
Princess Ashley, 1987
Those Summer Girls I Never Met, 1988
Voices After Midnight, 1989

Unfinished Portrait of Jessica, 1991
Bel-Air Bambi and the Mall Rats, 1993
The Last Safe Place on Earth, 1995
Lost in Cyberspace, 1995
The Great Interactive Dream Machine: Another Adventure in Cyberspace, 1996
Strays Like Us, 1998
A Long Way from Chicago, 1998
Amanda/Miranda, 1999 (abridged version; taken from the 1980 novel of the same name)
A Year Down Yonder, 2000
Fair Weather, 2001

Novels for Adults

Amanda/Miranda, 1980 (republished in an abridged version for young adults in 1999)
New York Times, 1981
This Family of Women, 1983
London Holiday, 1998

Other

Old Town, A Complete Guide: Strolling, Shopping, Supping, Sipping, 1965, with Norman Strasma (guidebook)
Sounds and Silences: Poetry for Now, 1970 (editor)
Mindscapes: Poems for the Real World, 1971 (editor)
Pictures that Storm Inside My Head: Poems for the Inner You, 1976 (editor)
Monster Night at Grandma's House, 1977, with Don Freeman (children's picture book)
Anonymously Yours, 1991 (autobiography)

HONORS AND AWARDS

National Council for the Advancement of Education Writing Award: 1971
Edgar Allan Poe Mystery Award (Mystery Writers of America): 1973, for *Dreamland Lake*; 1977, for *Are You in the House Alone?*
Best Book for Young Adults (American Library Association): 1974, for *Representing Superdoll*; 1976, for *Are You in the House Alone?*; 1977, for *Ghosts I Have Been*; 1978, for *Father Figure*; 1981, for *Close Enough to Touch*; 1987, for *Princess Ashley*; 2001, *A Year Down Yonder*
Notable Books for Children (American Library Association): 1975, for *The Ghost Belonged to Me*; 1986, for *Blossom Culp and the Sleep of Death*; 1987, for *Princess Ashley*; 2001, *A Year Down Yonder*

Friends of American Writers Award: 1976, for *The Ghost Belonged to Me*
Best Books of the Year (*School Library Journal*): 1976, for *Are You in the House Alone?*; 1977, for *Ghosts I Have Been*
Outstanding Books of the Year (*New York Times*): 1977, for *Ghosts I Have Been*
Best of the Best Books 1970-1982 (American Library Association): *Father Figure, Ghosts I Have Been, Are You in the House Alone?*
ALAN Award (National Council of Teachers of English: 1990, for outstanding contributions to young adult literature
Margaret Edwards Young Adult Author Achievement Award (American Library Association): 1990, honoring lifetime achievement in writing for young adults
Newbery Medal: 2001, for *A Year Down Yonder*

FURTHER READING

Books

Contemporary Authors, Vols. 85-88
Contemporary Authors New Revision Series, Vol. 19
Gallo, Donald R. *Presenting Richard Peck*, 1989
Holtze, Sally Holmes. *Fifth Book of Junior Authors and Illustrators*, 1983
Something About the Author Autobiography Series, Vol. 2, 1986
Twentieth-Century Children's Writers, 1989
Twentieth-Century Young Adult Writers, 1994
Writers for Young Adults, Vol. 3, 1997
Who's Who in America, 2001

Periodicals

Arkansas Libraries, Dec. 1981, p.13
Book, Jan. 2001, p.83
Book Report, Mar./Apr. 1992, p.40; Jan./Feb. 1999, p.64
Booklist, May 1, 1994, p.1611; Sep. 1, 1996, p.131; Apr. 1998, p.1325
Bulletin of the Center for Children's Books, Mar. 1977, p.111; Nov. 1981, p.53
Chicago Tribune, Apr. 19, 2000, p.4 (Trib West section)
Horn Book Magazine, Nov. 1998, p.738; July/Aug. 2001, p.397; July/Aug. 2001, p.403
Kirkus Reviews, May 1, 1987, p.723
New York Times Book Review, Nov. 12, 1972, p.8; Jan. 13, 1974, p.10; Nov. 14, 1976, p.29
Phoenix Arizona Republic, Nov. 29, 1999, p.D8
Pittsburgh Post-Gazette, May 8, 2001, p.E2

Publishers Weekly, Mar. 14, 1980, p.6; July 17, 1978, p.168
San Antonio Express-News, Mar. 25, 2001, p.J5
Scholastic Voice, Sep. 6, 1985, p.12
School Library Journal, Sep. 1981, p.140; Aug. 1987, p.97; June 1990, p.36; May 1998, p.147
St. Petersburg Times, Mar. 3, 1990, p.1 (City Times section)
Top of the News, Spring 1987, p.297
Ventura County (Calif.) Star, Jan. 12, 2001, p.E1
Voice of Youth Advocates, Oct. 1981, p.36; June 1987, p.82

Other

"All Things Considered," National Public Radio, Jan.15, 2001, program transcript

ADDRESS

Delacorte Press
1 Dag Hammarskjold Plaza
New York, NY 10017

WORLD WIDE WEB SITES

http://www.randomhouse.com/teachers/authors/peck.html
http://teacher.scholastic.com/authorsandbooks/events/peck/

Andrea Davis Pinkney 1963-

American Children's Book Writer and Editor
Author of *Hold Fast to Dreams, Raven in a Dove House, Silent Thunder: A Civil War Story*, and *Let It Shine: Stories of Black Women Freedom Fighters*

BIRTH

Andrea Davis Pinkney was born on September 25, 1963, in Washington, D.C. She was one of three children in her family.

YOUTH

Pinkney was born during the civil rights movement, a national drive to end segregation and gain equal rights for black people in American society. One of the key events of the civil rights movement was a 1963 demonstration known as the March on Washington. Pinkney's father attended this event and saw Dr. Martin Luther King Jr. give his famous "I Have a Dream" speech. But her mother, who was eight months pregnant with Andrea at the time, stayed in their nearby apartment and watched the event on television. "Mom says I kicked and squirmed inside her belly throughout Dr. King's powerful speech," Pinkney noted. "And though I was yet to be born, the March on Washington became my earliest experience with the civil rights movement."

When Pinkney was a child, her family moved from Washington to the mostly white suburb of Wilton, Connecticut. Throughout her childhood in Wilton, she enjoyed reading and writing stories. "My mother was a grade school teacher. She read books all the time. And my father was and still is a very good storyteller. And growing up in their house was what inspired me to choose a career in which I write books," she explained. "My favorite authors growing up were Judy Blume and Chaim Potok. And when I was a little girl I liked *Curious George* by H.A. Rey and anything by Ezra Jack Keats."

"My mother was a grade school teacher. She read books all the time. And my father was and still is a very good storyteller. And growing up in their house was what inspired me to choose a career in which I write books. My favorite authors growing up were Judy Blume and Chaim Potok. And when I was a little girl I liked Curious George *by H.A. Rey and anything by Ezra Jack Keats."*

Pinkney's family often told stories around the dinner table, and Andrea wrote her first story in the second grade. Her mother also shared her love of the performing arts with the children, taking them to New York City to see the ballet and the Alvin Ailey Dance Company. In addition to her literary and cultural experiences, however, Pinkney was influenced by television. "I also watched two television shows that had a great effect on me," she recalled. "One was 'The Waltons.' The eldest son, John Boy, was a writer, and my favorite part of the program was when he would read from his journal about life on Walton's Mountain at the beginning and the end of each show. I also loved 'The Mary Tyler Moore Show.' Mary was a journalist who lived in a big city, and I looked at her and thought, 'That's it, that's what I want to be.'"

EDUCATION

Pinkney was a good student throughout her school years in Wilton. In high school, she enjoyed working on the student newspaper. She attended Syracuse University in New York, where she started out studying performing arts with the goal of becoming a professional dancer. But she soon realized that writing was her first love and changed her major to journalism. She graduated from Syracuse with a bachelor's degree in journalism in 1985.

CAREER HIGHLIGHTS

Pinkney is the author of 15 books for children and young adults. Some of her best-known works are her picture books, several of which have been illustrated by her husband, Brian Pinkney. The Pinkneys have worked together to produce four critically acclaimed children's biographies of African-Americans who have made unique contributions to science, entertainment, or the arts.

Andrea Davis Pinkney's works also include four young adult novels and one nonfiction book for young adults. *Hold Fast to Dreams* and *Raven in a Dove House* are contemporary novels based upon her own experiences growing up, while *Silent Thunder* is a historical novel that follows the lives of two young slaves during the Civil War. *Let It Shine: Stories of Black Women Freedom Fighters* is a collection of short biographies of ten African-American women who played an active role in the fight for equal rights. Her most recent book, *Abraham Lincoln: Letters from a Slave Girl,* is an historical novel in the form of letters.

Starting Out as a Journalist and Editor

Before she began writing her own books, however, Pinkney started out as a journalist and as an editor in the field of children's book publishing. Immediately after she graduated from college, Pinkney moved to New York City and worked as an editor at several magazines. It was during this time that she met her future husband, Brian Pinkney, who was also working in magazine publishing. Brian's parents are the award-winning illustrator Jerry Pinkney and the well-known children's book author Gloria Pinkney.

After working at other magazine jobs, Andrea got a job at *Essence,* a magazine aimed at African-American women. There she wrote feature articles and managed the modern living section. But she also became interested in the field of children's books during this time. "While I worked at *Essence,* I

would watch Brian create books for children," she remembered. "And I would think that's something that I would really love to do."

In the early 1990s, Pinkney made the jump from magazine publishing to book publishing. She worked at the Simon and Schuster publishing house for a while, and then became an editor at Hyperion Books for Children. As a children's book editor, Pinkney became known for promoting the works of African-American writers and publishing stories that provided positive role models for black readers. At Hyperion, she eventually had the opportunity to form her own imprint, a separate line of books with a specific focus. Her imprint focuses on books for African-American children.

Pinkney named the new imprint Jump at the Sun, after a story by Zora Neale Hurston in which her mother told her "to aim high in life—to jump at the sun." "This line of books celebrates the beauty of black culture while at the same time inviting all readers to enjoy this special cultural experience," Pinkney explained. "Our message is for the child of color. . . . We want them to say this book is about me—it's for me. Yes, I count in this world."

In 2001, Pinkney was named editor-in-chief of Disney Books for Young Readers (Hyperion is a division of Disney). She thus became the first black woman to take charge of a mainstream children's book division. In this position, she oversees the publication of 80 titles per year. She also continues to lead the Jump in the Sun imprint, which has published books by such respected writers as Toni Morrison, Bell Hooks, Eloise Greenfield, and Veronica Chambers.

"This line of books celebrates the beauty of black culture while at the same time inviting all readers to enjoy this special cultural experience. Our message is for the child of color. . . . We want them to say this book is about me—it's for me. Yes, I count in this world."

Writing Her Own Children's Books

As Pinkney established herself as an editor of children's books, her husband's career as an illustrator also blossomed. Brian kept encouraging Andrea to write her own books, but she wanted her first effort as an author to be a joint project. After looking into several possible projects over the years, the couple finally agreed to create a children's biography of Alvin Ailey, a dancer and choreographer who explored the black experience through movement. Their picture book *Alvin Ailey* was published in 1993.

Over the next few years, the Pinkneys published several more biographies of notable African-Americans. Andrea Pinkney does a great deal of research in the process of writing her biographies. In addition to collecting materials from the library, she visits historic sites and talks with family members, descendants, and other people who knew the subjects. As a result, her biographies both capture the personalities of their subjects and show their contributions to society.

For example, *Dear Benjamin Banneker,* published in 1994, tells the story of a free black man who lived in the 18th century. Banneker taught himself astronomy, published an almanac, and corresponded with Thomas Jefferson about ending the practice of slavery in the United States. *Bill Picket: Rodeo-Ridin' Cowboy,* published in 1996, tells the story of an African-American rodeo cowboy who came up with a unique method of controlling bulls.

> "
>
> *The Pinkneys enjoy working together, as Brian Pinkney explains here. "It has to be something we're both excited about. Usually that means there is some aspect that adds something for me in terms of the visuals. Then we bounce it back and forth in terms of the direction it may go in. Sometimes Andrea may do a rough draft first, and I'll read that and have some comments on it. Other times we'll sit down and maybe I'll lay out some thumbnail sketches of the way I see images going. And then Andrea has that as a structure for the story."*
>
> "

Duke Ellington: The Piano Prince and His Orchestra, published in 1998, is an award-winning biography of a famous jazz musician and bandleader of the 1930s and 1940s. "A tantalizing combination of sassy prose and swinging artistry, this electrifying picture-book biography of one of the biggest stars in the musical constellation jumps and jives to a palpable beat," wrote a *Publishers Weekly* reviewer. "Andrea Davis Pinkney's jaunty, slangy text tells a story and does it with a rhythm and style that manage to capture Ellington's era without sounding silly to today's kids," Bill Ott added in *Booklist. Duke Ellington: The Piano Prince and His Orchestra* was named a Caldecott Honor Book and a Coretta Scott King Honor Book, both for illustration.

Pinkney has also worked with her husband to produce several other picture books, including *Seven Candles for Kwanzaa* (1993), *Shake, Shake, Shake* (1997), and *Watch Me Dance* (1997). The Pinkneys enjoy having the opportunity to work together. "It has to be something we're both excited about," Brian said of their joint projects. "Usually that means there is some aspect that adds something for me in terms of the visuals. Then we bounce it back and forth in terms of the direction it may go in. Sometimes Andrea may do a rough draft first, and I'll read that and have some comments on it. Other times we'll sit down and maybe I'll lay out some thumbnail sketches of the way I see images going. And then Andrea has that as a structure for the story."

Novels for Young Adults

In addition to her children's books, Pinkney has also written several books for young adults. Two of these books, *Hold Fast to Dreams* and *Raven in a Dove House,* are contemporary novels based on her own experiences growing up. The stories feature African-American girls who struggle to develop a sense of their own identity within a new community.

Hold Fast to Dreams, published in 1995, tells the story of Dee, a 12-year-old girl whose family moves from Baltimore to Wexford, Connecticut, when her father gets a better job. "*Hold Fast to Dreams* came from an article that I wrote for the *New York Times,*" Pinkney recalled. "It was an article based on my personal experience of growing up in a small town in Connecticut where there were very few black families. The article is very short. But I always knew there was a longer story to tell." In the novel, Dee suddenly finds herself in a new school where she is the only black girl. None of her classmates has ever heard of Langston Hughes, her favorite poet. And everyone is crazy about lacrosse, a sport that she is not well-suited to play. Dee's father and younger sister also struggle to fit in to their new community. "In a straightforward, first-person narrative, Pinkney tells a truthful story of a 12-year-old's adjustment to new and different surroundings and of a black family's pursuit of the American dream," Lauren Adams noted in a review for *Horn Book.* "Frank dialogue about how white kids and black kids view each other helps to burst apart stereotypes while affirming racial difference," added a reviewer for *Publishers Weekly.*

Pinkney's next young adult novel, *Raven in a Dove House,* was published in 1998. It tells the story of Nell, a 12-year-old girl who spends the summer with her aunt in the small town of Modine, New York. At first, she has fun hanging out with her 14-year-old cousin, Foley. She also develops a crush on her cousin's cool best friend, Slade. She is thrilled when she receives her first kiss from Slade. But then the boys talk Nell into hiding a "raven" pistol in her old doll house. Nell feels uneasy about the gun and has bad dreams about it. As the story unfolds, the pistol creates a tragedy, just as she had feared. In the end, however, the tragic event pulls her family closer together. "Grim foreshadowing adds weight and texture to this poignant and ultimately uplifting coming-of-age story," said a *Publishers Weekly* reviewer.

In 1999, Pinkney published a historical novel for young adults. *Silent Thunder: A Civil War Story* is told from the perspective of two young African-

American slaves—11-year-old Summer and her older brother, Rosco—who live on a Virginia plantation in 1862. Rosco, who works as the personal servant of the master's young son, learns to read by eavesdropping on the boy's school lessons. He also learns that President Abraham Lincoln has issued the Emancipation Proclamation, which declared that slaves held in states that supported the South in the Civil War were free. Slave owners tried to prevent slaves from learning to read or hearing about Lincoln's order. They feared that such knowledge would encourage the slaves to try to escape. So Rosco and Summer must conceal this information, as well as their own feelings and desires.

Critics praised *Silent Thunder* for showing readers what life might have been like for young people under slavery. "As Summer and Rosco alternate as narrators, their feelings flow off the page to envelop the reader," noted a reviewer for *Publishers Weekly*. "The individual characters, both black and white, are drawn with complexity as the compelling story reveals the intricate connections between them," Hazel Rochman added in *Booklist*.

Recent Books

In 2000, Pinkney published *Let It Shine: Stories of Black Women Freedom Fighters*. It includes biographies of ten African-American women who overcame fear and prejudice to join the fight for freedom and equality. Some of the featured women include Harriet Tubman, Sojourner Truth, Rosa Parks, and Shirley Chisholm. "Blending straightforward narrative with a lively storytelling style, the author balances the hardships and racial injustice that these women faced against their faith, strength of character, and determination," Marie Orlando wrote in *School Library Journal*.

Pinkney drew upon her own interest in black history and the civil rights movement in writing *Let It Shine,* which she said covers "the challenges and triumphs of civil rights that spanned American history from the 18th

century to the present day." She hopes that the biographies of prominent African-American women inspire young readers to stand up for their own beliefs. These stories "reflect something in each of us," she stated. "The courage to fight for what we believe is right, the willingness to stand up under fire and disadvantage, the serenity to carry on when self-doubt, weariness, and the ignorance of others stand in the way of progress, and the fortitude to keep one's eyes on those prizes that will lead to a better world." For *Let It Shine: Stories of Black Women Freedom Fighters,* Pinkney received the Coretta Scott King Honor in 2001.

Pinkney tried something a little different in her next book, *Abraham Lincoln: Letters from a Slave Girl* (2001). This book is part of the Dear Mr. President Series, which uses a fictionalized exchange of letters between a young person and a U.S. president to profile the president and to illuminate important events of the era. In *Abraham Lincoln: Letters from a Slave Girl,* Pinkney includes fictionalized letters between President Lincoln and Lettie Tucker, a 12-year-old slave girl on a plantation in Charleston, South Carolina. Lettie writes about the circumstances of her life and challenges the president on the issue of slavery, while Lincoln responds with details on life in the White House and the progress of the Civil War. This lively two-year correspondence, combined with photos, paintings, and other reproductions, brings history to life.

Pinkney continues to work full-time as a children's book editor and publishing executive. But she enjoys writing her own books so much that she still manages to find time to do it. She often comes up with book ideas while she is daydreaming on the subway on her way to work. She writes the ideas down in a notebook that she carries in her purse, then transfers them to her computer later. She does most of her actual writing on the weekends, when her daughter is taking a nap. "I can't say it isn't hard. There are times I don't feel like it or I want to do something else, but I tell myself, This is the only time you have, so you better do it," she stated. "A writer is just who I am."

"

The inspirational stories in Let It Shine *"reflect something in each of us. The courage to fight for what we believe is right, the willingness to stand up under fire and disadvantage, the serenity to carry on when self-doubt, weariness, and the ignorance of others stand in the way of progress, and the fortitude to keep one's eyes on those prizes that will lead to a better world."*

"

MARRIAGE AND FAMILY

Andrea Davis married artist and illustrator Brian Pinkney in 1991. The couple met in 1986, when they were both working for magazines early in their careers—Andrea at *Mechanics Illustrated,* and Brian at *Field and Stream.* "We laugh about that now," she stated. "We weren't particularly interested in either mechanics or fields and streams, but we both wanted to get to New York, and those places were where we found jobs." The Pinkneys have one daughter and live in an apartment in Brooklyn, New York.

HOBBIES AND OTHER INTERESTS

When she is not writing, Pinkney enjoys singing and dancing. She dreams about someday becoming a singer and appearing on Broadway.

WRITINGS

Books for Children

Alvin Ailey, 1993
Seven Candles for Kwanzaa, 1993
Dear Benjamin Banneker, 1994
Bill Picket: Rodeo-Ridin' Cowboy, 1996
I Smell Honey, 1997
Pretty Brown Face, 1997
Shake, Shake, Shake, 1997
Solo Girl, 1997
Watch Me Dance, 1997
Duke Ellington: The Piano Prince and His Orchestra, 1998
Belly-Hum Christmas, 2000

Books for Young Adults

Hold Fast to Dreams, 1995
Raven in a Dove House, 1998
Silent Thunder: A Civil War Story, 1999
Let It Shine: Stories of Black Women Freedom Fighters, 2000
Abraham Lincoln: Letters from a Slave Girl, 2001

HONORS AND AWARDS

Best Arts Feature Award (Highlights for Children Foundation): 1992
Parenting Publication Award: 1993

FURTHER READING

Books

Contemporary Authors, Vol. 185, 2000
Something about the Author, Vol. 113, 2000
St. James Guide to Children's Writers, 1999

Periodicals

Booklist, Feb. 15, 1995, p.1085; June 1, 1998, p.1757; Feb. 15, 1998, p.1000; Feb. 15, 1999, p.1056; Sep. 1, 1999, p.134; Nov. 15, 2000, p.637
Fresno (Calif.) Bee, Feb. 21, 1999, p.E3
Horn Book, Sep.-Oct. 1995, p.602; Jan. 11, 1996, p.42; Nov. 2000, p.77C
New York Times, Sep. 25, 1994, Westchester sec., p.23
Publishers Weekly, May 22, 1995, p.60; Feb. 2, 1998, p.91; Mar. 2, 1998, p.68; Oct. 4, 1999, p.76; Sep. 11, 2000, p.92
School Library Journal, Oct. 2000, p.190
Teaching K-8, Vol. 28, No. 2, 1997, p.38

ADDRESS

Hyperion Books for Children
114 Fifth Avenue
New York, NY 10011

WORLD WIDE WEB SITE

http://www.disney.go.com/educational/transcript.htm

Louise Rennison 1951?-

British Comedian and Writer
Author of *Angus, Thongs and Full-Frontal Snogging* and *On the Bright Side, I'm Now the Girlfriend of a Sex God*

BIRTH

Louise Rennison was born in Leeds, England, around 1951. Her family came from Irish and Jewish backgrounds. She has a sister, Sophie, who is 11 years younger.

YOUTH

Rennison grew up in Leeds, where she lived in a three-bedroom house with various members of her extended family.

"My parents and I had one bedroom, my grandparents had another, and my aunt, uncle, and cousin had the last one," she recalled. "It was certainly a very full house." Although her family did not have much money, they still managed to have a lot of fun. "I had a very fun childhood," she remembered. "My family all had quite a good sense of humor, we were encouraged to have a laugh. It was very free and happy."

Rennison enjoyed reading as a child. "I used to read anything that was around. We weren't very wealthy and I used to get loads of secondhand books from a cousin," she noted. "I also read girls' mags and James Bond books." She also liked going to football (soccer) games with her father. Rennison, who has worked as an actress and stand-up comedian, first started performing in front of her parents' friends. "My parents used to go out on Friday nights and drink Guinness [beer] and rediscover their Irish roots," she recalled. "They'd get me to dance on the table. Middle-class children get taught piano. Irish dancing was my education."

Although her family did not have much money, they still managed to have a lot of fun. "I had a very fun childhood. My family all had quite a good sense of humor, we were encouraged to have a laugh. It was very free and happy."

When Rennison was 15, her family moved to Wairakei, New Zealand. She hated New Zealand and missed her friends and her active social life back home. "There were more sheep than people and they were a lot more interesting and wanted to go out more," she remembered. Rennison complained about the situation so much that her parents finally agreed to send her back to England to live with her grandparents. "I did actually come back quite swiftly anyway because I made my parents' lives such misery in New Zealand," she admitted. "I used to lie in the garden saying, 'Now you've ruined my life, what are you going to do about it?' My poor mother had to get two jobs to pay for my fare back to England, I think!"

EDUCATION

Like Georgia Nicolson—the main character in her popular novels—Rennison attended an all-girls' prep school and had to wear a school uniform. "Our uniform was navy blue with a gold emblem and the beret was also navy blue," she recalled. "I'm sorry but nobody looks good in a beret—not even the French. Like Georgia, we did the 'rolling the beret up like a thin sausage and sticking it under our hair' trick."

Rennison has both pleasant and unpleasant memories of her school days. She had a close circle of friends and enjoyed a busy social life. But she also had her share of teenage problems and insecurities. "There were so many days at school that were torture, like having to go into school without having done your homework and being made to feel inadequate and insecure and stupid," she noted. "I am most grateful for meeting kindred spirits at school though; lots of people don't. I still love those friends."

——— " ———

"There were so many days at school that were torture, like having to go into school without having done your homework and being made to feel inadequate and insecure and stupid. I am most grateful for meeting kindred spirits at school though; lots of people don't. I still love those friends."

Rennison took some time off from school in her 20s. But she eventually returned to school to take courses in expressive arts at Brighton University. In one memorable course, her tutor came up to her after a performance and told her that she should never go on stage again because her acting made him physically ill. But the negative feedback only made Rennison more determined to succeed. "I could never be nervous about doing anything after that course," she stated.

FIRST JOBS

Shortly after she completed her education at the all-girls' school, Rennison moved to London with some of her friends. She spent the next dozen years in the middle of the city's busy social scene—hanging out with various bands, working at odd jobs, and traveling whenever the opportunity arose. "I went to live in London in the 1970s. I happened to end up living in Notting Hill Gate in a one-bedroom flat owned by [the rock band] Roxy Music," she recalled. "At night we used to go to a real nutter's pub called the Prince of Wales, where [the rock band] Pink Floyd used to hang out. It was a really funny time." When Rennison was 17, she dated a boy who was a member of a band and ended up getting pregnant. She had the baby and then gave it up for adoption.

Rennison spent most of her 20s in London, which was home to many famous musicians during that time. Over the years, she met Pete Townshend, Rod Stewart, Bryan Ferry, Cat Stevens, Stevie Wonder, and the members of Led Zeppelin, among many other famous people. One time, when she was backstage during a Pink Floyd concert, one of the band's special effects went haywire. While fleeing a flying rocket, Rennison ended up running onto the stage. "There was me, the celebrities, and the caterers trying to get away and I was forced onstage in front of thousands of people," she remembered. "I'd got these massive lights on me, so I did the only thing I knew how to do and started Irish dancing."

During her early years in London, Rennison had a job building recreational equipment for children in poor areas of the city. Unfortunately, the underprivileged kids did not appreciate her efforts. "We used to build these jungle gyms and tree houses for them, and they'd watch, and then just take them all down again, or set fire to them," she recalled. "Actually, one of them set fire to my friend's jumper—while she was wearing it. It was very humiliating."

BECOMING A WRITER

In the 1980s, Rennison began writing funny stories about her experiences meeting famous people and following rock bands on tour. She published a few stories in magazines, which led to jobs writing jokes for well-known British comedians. After attending classes at Brighton University, Rennison developed her own one-woman, stand-up comedy show—"Stevie Wonder Felt My Face"—based on her youthful experiences. "It was a kind of monologue, a rite-of-passage show about growing up," she explained. Rennison made her debut as a stand-up comedian in 1991 at the Edinburgh Comedy Festival in Scotland, where she beat out several well-known comedians for the top prize. "Stevie Wonder Felt My Face" earned great reviews, ran for four years, and was adapted for BBC television.

Following the success of her first one-woman show, Rennison created and appeared in two other original comedy routines, "Bob Marley's Gardener Sold My Friend" and "Never Eat Anything Bigger Than Your Head." By the mid-1990s, she was also writing a humorous column for the *London Evening Standard* and providing commentary for radio shows. "I used to do these segments for 'Home Truths' and 'Woman's Hour' on Radio 4," she recalled. "They would be about things like me buying shoes that were too small just because they were pretty. Often, the stories were true. I did buy these strappy stilettos and I wore them out on a night with my boyfriend but we had a fight and I stormed off. I walked for ages and ages because I got lost and the straps on my shoes started cutting into my feet really badly. I ended up going to hospital because the straps were just embedded in my flesh and there was no way I could take the shoes off. I was wailing,

'Can you save them? Please save them,' and they thought I meant my feet."

In the late 1990s, an editor from the Piccadilly Press publishing house read one of Rennison's newspaper columns. Entitled "Dating Over 35," it provided a humorous look at the hopelessness of the London dating scene for women approaching middle age. After reading the article, the editor surprised Rennison by asking her to write a young adult novel. "An English publisher read my article and phoned up and said they loved it and would I consider doing a book for them," Rennison remembered. "I was very flattered and imagined that they meant a sort of sophisticated girl about town thing. She said, no they thought a teenage girl's diary. I said, 'Er . . . why me?' And the [editor] said, 'Because I have never read anything so self-obsessed and childish.'" Rennison was intrigued by the idea and began working on a book, which turned into her best-selling young adult novel *Angus, Thongs and Full-Frontal Snogging: Confessions of Georgia Nicolson.*

"

"An English publisher read my article and phoned up and said they loved it and would I consider doing a book for them. I was very flattered and imagined that they meant a sort of sophisticated girl about town thing. She said, no they thought a teenage girl's diary. I said, 'Er . . . why me?' And the [editor] said, 'Because I have never read anything so self-obsessed and childish.'"

"

CAREER HIGHLIGHTS

Angus, Thongs and Full-Frontal Snogging

Angus, Thongs and Full-Frontal Snogging, published in 1999, is the fictional diary of Georgia Nicolson, a 14-year-old British schoolgirl. Georgia's daily life is filled with amusing misadventures, which she relates with her own cheeky brand of charm. Rennison has said that nearly all of the incidents that take place in the book were drawn from her own experiences as a teenager. "Almost everything that happened in the books happened to me and, yes, I am including shaving off my eyebrows, which was the act of a complete and utter prat [idiot]," she admitted. Like Georgia, Rennison also tended to run away when she was embarrassed, spoke French all the time, humiliated herself by attending a party dressed as a stuffed olive, and took snogging (kissing) lessons from an older boy. "Sadly the bit in the

LOUISE RENNISON
ANGUS, thongs and FULL-FRONTAL SNOGGING
confessions of
Georgia Nicolson

book about the snogging lesson is actually true," she noted. "I think the boy actually volunteered for the job. We would queue up [stand in line] and then have half an hour with him; he used to time it!"

All of the characters in Rennison's novel are based on real people. In fact, she even used the real names of people she knew growing up. "I may as well come clean now," she stated. "When I wrote the books I based all of my characters on real people—Sex God, Wet Lindsay, Slim, Herr Kamyer, Elvis Attwood—and I used their real names in the writing, intending to change them before publication. But I forgot, so I am expecting to be killed when I go back to my hometown." Even Georgia's cat, Angus, is based on one of Rennison's childhood pets. "Angus is real as well," she explained. "I absolutely loved him. He was the best cat known to humanity and he really did beat up next doors' poodles—they had to be sent to an animal psychologist in the end because they wouldn't come out of the house."

"

Nearly all of the incidents that take place in Angus, Thongs and Full-Frontal Snogging *were drawn from Rennison's own experiences as a teenager. "Almost everything that happened in the books happened to me and, yes, I am including shaving off my eyebrows, which was the act of a complete and utter prat [idiot]."*

Georgia, the main character in *Angus, Thongs and Full-Frontal Snogging,* is loosely based on Rennison herself. "Most of the character is from my own rather feverish memory of being a teenager," she noted. "The sense of humor is definitely me. I did spend most of my teenage years helpless with laughter, usually at the most inappropriate moments." At the same time, Rennison did consciously create a character separate from herself when she began writing in Georgia's voice. "I wanted Georgia to be a decent person," she explained. "I wanted her to be someone who is a bit stupid and self-obsessed and difficult and funny and rude, and a bit jealous and all those other things. But I wanted her to have a good heart."

Rennison's first novel was an immediate hit with readers and critics alike. *Angus, Thongs and Full-Frontal Snogging* became a best-seller in England shortly after it was published, and the same thing occurred a few months later when it appeared in the United States. In a review for *School Library Journal,* Angela J. Reynolds said Rennison's novel was "fresh, lively, and engaging." A reviewer for *Publishers Weekly* called the book "a spectacular YA debut." Writing in *Booklist,* Michael Cart noted that "Georgia is a wonderful character whose misadventures are not only hysterically funny but universally recognizable. This 'fabbity, fab, fab' novel will leave readers cheering . . . and anxiously awaiting the promised sequel."

Book Creates Controversy

Despite the positive reviews and enthusiastic reader response, however, *Angus, Thongs and Full-Frontal Snogging* also created some controversy. It was nominated for the Smarties Prize — one of the premier British awards for children's literature — in the category of books for nine- to 11-year-old readers. Nominees for the prize are selected by a panel of adult experts, then the winners are selected by students. But some parents and teachers felt that Rennison's novel included too much sexual content for the age group. As a result, two schools pulled out of the judging rather than allow their students to read it.

"I wanted Georgia to be a decent person. I wanted her to be someone who is a bit stupid and self-obsessed and difficult and funny and rude, and a bit jealous and all those other things. But I wanted her to have a good heart."

Rennison acknowledges that her novel includes some discussion of sexual matters. For example, Georgia obsesses about boys, worries about the size of her breasts, and thinks that her nasty female gym teacher is a lesbian. But the author says that she did not intend to shock or offend anyone with her book. "If you are writing spontaneously you are not necessarily thinking about your audience, your moral standpoint, or how somebody would feel if they read your work, you are just involved in creating something," she stated. "I wrote the book for me and I didn't expect it to be put into a category for nine to 11-year-olds. I do think that children are self-censoring when they read books, however. I think that if something was not interesting to them they just wouldn't read it. If they didn't know what lesbians were they just wouldn't be interested. So I don't think there is any danger of me making anyone into a lesbian or anything or making them go snog someone before they are inclined to."

Rennison also finds great value in novels that discuss sexual issues of concern to teens in an honest and understanding way. "I would have loved to

have books like this around when I was younger. I used to stick my fingers in my ears in Biology — the idea of a teacher standing around and talking about this stuff just made me cringe — still does! I would've loved some outside information about sex and boys. We were completely clueless," she noted. "If I had had a sister like Georgia when I was little who had a sort of funny attitude toward sexual things and talked about it, it would have been great."

An International Phenomenon

Despite the controversy in England, Rennison's novel became a huge success in the United States, with specialists in children's literature as well as young readers. The novel won a variety of awards in the U.S. and was named a Michael L. Printz Honor Book, a runner up for the prestigious award given by the American Library Association to the year's best book for young adults. The book became so popular, in fact, that countless American teenagers began to adopt the British slang words that Georgia and her friends use in the book. "Teenagers really love something that's theirs, something secret," she explained. "I think that's why they've adopted Georgia's language." Rennison uses so many slang terms that she had to provide a glossary in U.S. editions of her novel. Some examples include: "fringe," which describes a goofy bit of short hair above the eyebrows (bangs); "naff," which means embarrassingly and hopelessly out of fashion; and "prat," which entails making a ridiculous fool of yourself.

"The slang I use is partly made up and partly what we used at school and partly what me and my friends use now. It's fantastic actually because it has become a real cult over here [in England], all over the country girls are calling their dads Vati and asking if they can go to the piddly diddly department [restroom]. Even more fab is that I have now started getting letters from American girls saying that they are 'practicing being British' and can I send them any more British words so that they can get really good at it!"

"The slang I use is partly made up and partly what we used at school and partly what me and my friends use now," Rennison noted. "It's fantastic actually because it has become a real cult over here [in England], all over the country girls are calling their dads Vati and asking if they can go to the piddly diddly department [restroom]. Even more fab is that I have now started getting letters from American girls saying that they are 'practicing being British' and can I send them any more British words so that they can get really good at it!" She enjoys hearing from her American fans, although she is sometimes baffled by their requests. "What really gets me is that they ask for a 'British to English translation,'" she laughed.

"

"The thing about being a teenager is you do these things to try to look good—they nearly always fail and you have to go to school looking a disaster. At one point I took vitamin A pills which were supposed to give you 'a glowing all-over tan'—everything went orange, even my poo! I also made the mistake of having a home perm—which was a disaster. . . . I hated it so much I attacked it with a pair of scissors until it was only a couple of inches long. It looked like a chicken had cut it."

"

Continuing Georgia's Story

Following the success of her first book, Rennison wrote two more novels about Georgia. She continued to draw upon her own comic experiences as a teenager in her second book, published in England in 2000 as *It's OK, I'm Wearing Really Big Knickers: Further Confessions of Georgia Nicolson* and republished in 2001 in the United States as *On the Bright Side, I'm Now the Girlfriend of a Sex God: Further Confessions of Georgia Nicolson*. For example, the author made her character try out some of her own failed beauty secrets. "The thing about being a teenager is you do these things to try to look good—they nearly always fail and you have to go to school looking a disaster. At one point I took vitamin A pills which were supposed to give you 'a glowing all-over tan'—everything went orange, even my poo!" she remembered. "I also made the mistake of having a home perm—which was a disaster. . . . I hated it so much I attacked it with a pair of scissors until it was only a couple of inches long. It looked like a chicken had cut it." In a departure from her real experiences, however, Rennison decided against sending her heroine to New Zealand. "I liked Georgia so much I couldn't make her go to that horrible place," she noted.

Both readers and critics enjoyed Rennison's sequel to her best-selling first novel. Writing in *School Library Journal,* Mara Bright called *On the Bright Side, I'm Now the Girlfriend of a Sex God* "a funny romp through the intricacies of one especially explosive period of growing up," and said that the book "will be devoured by girls on the brink of becoming teenagers and those who are in the thick of it now." A reviewer for *Horn Book* added that "Georgia is not exactly what you'd call likable; no one escapes her biting sarcasm—and it's this trenchant wit that makes her diary entries so entertaining."

Rennison's third book about Georgia, *Knocked Out by My Nunga-Nungas,* was published in England in 2001. It will soon be republished in the United States, but possibly under a new title. In this book, Georgia is a year older, but not too much wiser. "This anthem to misspent youth will strike a chord with all teenage girls and induce giggling nostalgia in their mothers," noted a reviewer for the *Sunday Mirror.*

The cover of the British edition of Rennison's third book about Georgia Nicolson.

FUTURE PLANS

Rennison has said in interviews that she may end her series of books about Georgia at three. She does plan to write more novels in the future, but she may target them at adults. She would also like to write a musical someday. In 2001, Rennison signed a contract with an American film production company to make a movie version of *Angus, Thongs and Full-Frontal Snogging.* She looks forward to being involved in the film, although she decided against writing the screenplay. "I had the chance to write the script but I thought, 'No, they can do it. I want to swan about on set throwing bits of advice in here and there!'" she recalled.

Rennison visited the United States in order to negotiate her movie deal. But the trip took longer than expected—she had to make the journey by boat due to her fear of flying. One of Rennison's plans for the future is overcoming this fear, as well as several others. "I'd like to get rid of my phobias. I am the phobia queen! I just get rid of one of them and then another pops up!" she said. "I can't fly and in fact they had to abort a take-off so that I could leave the plane I was supposed to be traveling to America on. Then I got on the boat and found that I was phobic on boats as well! Cabin too small, sea to wide, sky too low—you name it, I can be phobic about it! I think it is about time to get to grips with that!"

When she is at home in Brighton, England, Rennison writes 20 pages per day. At that rate, it takes her about six months to write a book. She wrote her first three novels "in a very eccentric place in the middle of town, called the Natural Health Centre," she stated. "I used to do yoga there."

ADVICE TO YOUNG WRITERS

Rennison is often asked to provide advice to aspiring young writers. "Don't try to write like anyone else. There's no right or wrong way. Find your own voice and don't be afraid if it's different from how other people write — that's a good thing," she noted. "Read loads of different magazines and newspapers, and send articles to the ones you like. I did that and eventually they started buying them!"

Rennison is often asked to provide advice to aspiring young writers. "Don't try to write like anyone else. There's no right or wrong way. Find your own voice and don't be afraid if it's different from how other people write — that's a good thing. Read loads of different magazines and newspapers, and send articles to the ones you like. I did that and eventually they started buying them!"

HOME AND FAMILY

Rennison lives in Brighton, England, with her boyfriend of three years, John. She also shares her home with two goldfish, Finn and Bjork. Today, Rennison is very close to her adult daughter, Kim O'Connor, whom she gave up for adoption as an infant. The two women met in the mid-1990s, when O'Connor began searching for her birth mother. A short time later, O'Connor moved from New Zealand to England to be closer to her mother. "It's strange, she's like my twin," Rennison said of her daughter. "She really annoyed me the other day and I said, 'God, she's so bloody selfish and superficial,' and my own mother just pointed at me."

HOBBIES AND OTHER INTERESTS

In her spare time, Rennison has said that she will usually "hang around with my mates, play tennis, go swimming, walk on the beach, gossip for hours on the telephone, and watch comedy." She is also a big fan of the Leeds United football (soccer) team.

WRITINGS

Angus, Thongs and Full-Frontal Snogging: Confessions of Georgia Nicolson, 1999 (British edition; published in the United States under the same title, 2000)

It's OK, I'm Wearing Really Big Knickers: Further Confessions of Georgia Nicolson, 2000 (British edition; published in the United States as *On the Bright Side, I'm Now the Girlfriend of a Sex God: Further Confessions of Georgia Nicolson,* 2001)

Knocked Out by My Nunga-Nungas: Further, Further Confessions of Georgia Nicolson, 2001 (British edition)

HONORS AND AWARDS

Nestle Smarties Children's Book Award Bronze Medal: 1999, for *Angus, Thongs and Full-Frontal Snogging*

Books for Youth Editor's Choice (*Booklist*): 2000, for *Angus, Thongs and Full-Frontal Snogging*

Notable Children's Book of the Year (American Library Association): 2001, for *Angus, Thongs and Full-Frontal Snogging*

Best Books for Young Adults (American Library Association): 2001, for *Angus, Thongs and Full-Frontal Snogging*

Quick Picks for Reluctant Young Readers (American Library Association): 2001, for *Angus, Thongs and Full-Frontal Snogging*

Books for the Teen Age (New York Public Library): 2001, for *Angus, Thongs and Full-Frontal Snogging*

FURTHER READING

Periodicals

Booklist, July 2000, p.2033; May 15, 2001, p.1751
Christian Science Monitor, Aug. 10, 2000, p.21
Daily Mail (London), Dec. 2, 1999, p.29; Aug. 23, 2001, p.56
Daily Telegraph (London), Nov. 13, 1999, p.5
Evening Standard (London), July 21, 1999, p.31
Express (London), July 16, 2001, p.17
Guardian (London), May 5, 1992, p.16
Horn Book, May 2000, p.320; May 2001, p.335
Publishers Weekly, Mar. 20, 2000, p.94; Feb. 26, 2001, p.87
School Library Journal, July 2000, p.109; May 2001, p.159
Scotsman (Edinburgh), Nov. 27, 1999, p.10; July 26, 2000, p.9
Sunday Mirror (London), July 22, 2001, p.42

ADDRESS

HarperCollins Publishers
10 East 53rd Street
New York, NY 10022

WORLD WIDE WEB SITES

http://www.schoolsnet.com
http://www.bookmagazine.com/archive/issue9/teenreads.shtml
http://news.bbc.co.uk/hi/english/uk/newsid_1443000/1443007.stm
http://www.bbc.co.uk/so/celeb/features/louise_rennison.shtml
http://www.teenreads.com/authors/au-rennison-louise.asp
http://www.alphabetstreet.infront.co.uk/Interviews/louiserennison.jhtml
http://www.thisisbrightonandhove.co.uk/brighton_hove/news_features/louise/rennison1.html

David Small 1945-

American Children's Book Author and Illustrator
Winner of the 2001 Caldecott Medal for *So You Want to Be President?*

BIRTH

David Small was born in Detroit, Michigan, on February 12, 1945. His father, Edward Pierce Small, was a doctor, and his mother, Elizabeth (Murphy) Small, was a homemaker.

YOUTH

Growing up in Detroit, Small was a bit of an outsider. He was very shy and had a hard time fitting in with the neighborhood children, who often called him names like "geek," "nerd," or "queer." In addition, Small was a sickly child. His various illnesses kept him in bed for long stretches of time. Since his family did not have a television until he was eight years old, he was forced to spend this quiet time alone, with just his imagination to keep him occupied.

As a way to pass the time, Small started drawing at a young age. Impressed by his skill, his mother encouraged his interest in drawing by enrolling him in Saturday morning art classes at the Detroit Institute of Arts. Unfortunately, Small soon became bored with the remedial curriculum that was offered in these classes. "How I loathed those lessons," he remembered. "They never taught me anything I was interested in, such as cartooning and drawing animals." Still, Small was captivated by the collection of masterpieces at the Detroit Institute of Arts. He particularly liked several murals by the famous Mexican painter Diego Rivera. These murals, which cover entire walls inside the museum, show scenes of the manufacturing activity for which Detroit is well known. 'That mural teaches you a respect for all humanity," he says. "All colors, all ethnicities are represented there. There's a tremendous nobility and respect for the common man." Viewing such works of art helped him learn that "that the work of an artist is noble and worthy, and that art—by changing the way we see—can direct our lives."

"

As a boy, Small found artistic inspiration in his father's office in the radiology department of a local hospital. "Many of my early memories are set in the X-ray department of that hospital, in those twilit rooms full of huge machines and glowing screens that revealed the insides of people. I can't help but think that those early encounters with people-as-skeletons encouraged my later interest in anatomy, as well as a rather dark creative vision."

"

As a boy, Small found artistic inspiration in some unlikely places. His father's office in the radiology department of a local hospital was one such place. "Many of my early memories are set in the X-ray department of that hospital, in those twilit rooms full of huge machines and glowing screens that revealed the insides of people," he noted. "I can't help but think that those early encounters with people-as-skeletons encouraged my later interest in anatomy, as well as a rather dark creative vision." Small also spent many summers at his grandparents' home in the Indiana countryside. It was there that his love for nature and his interest in sketching animals grew. Finally, he drew inspiration from popular cartoonists, including Walt Kelly, whose classic strip "Pogo" was Small's favorite. "I didn't get most of the politics, but I loved the way the character was drawn," he said.

EDUCATION

Small struggled in school and achieved only average grades. "I was a terrible student," he recalled, "painfully shy, much abused by the world around me, and unable for many years to be comfortable in it." The only subject that kept his interest was English. The art classes that Small took during his youth failed to inspire him. In elementary school, he was physically small, inept at sports, an outcast who was often picked on. "My school did not have the greatest arts program going, but at least it had one. If there had been no art room, no music, no school plays, an outsider like me would simply have been driven further and further underground. As it happened, because I was allowed to develop my art skills, by the end of seventh grade I wasn't being called those nasty names any more. Instead, the kids who used to call me a punk because I was bad at sports were calling me 'David Small, The Greatest Artist of Them All!' Of course I was only the greatest artist at MacDowell Elementary School, but this made me feel different about myself and was a beginning step in a new direction."

For a while, Small attended Cass Technical High School, a magnet school for talented students. But he hated the 45-minute bus trip to get there and the huge, impersonal size of the school. "I still have nightmares about getting lost in Cass Tech while trying to find my classroom," he says. He finished at Mumford High School, his local neighborhood school. Small was particularly interested in writing and the theater during high school. He thought he might become a playwright or an actor. He even had two plays produced by a small local company while he was still in high school.

After graduating from Mumford, Small attended Wayne State University in Detroit. At first, he planned to pursue a degree in English. But one day his roommate looked at some of the doodles and drawings in his notebook and suggested that he switch to an art major. "I'd never thought of art as a career because it was so easy and fun," he says. "I enjoyed writing, but writing was harder for me. Drawing was very natural. When I made that decision to switch [majors], it was as if a huge burden had been lifted."

Small finally found art classes that fully engaged his interest and creativity during his college years at Wayne State. He enrolled in drawing, painting, and printmaking classes and was overjoyed to be surrounded by instructors and other students who shared his passion for the arts. The experience changed his life. "I felt alive," he recalled. "I grew stronger. I knew that in this world of art I could find a place. The work never tired me. In fact, I couldn't find enough hours in the day to learn what I needed to know in order to make the kind of pictures I wanted to create." Small earned his bachelor of fine arts degree from Wayne State in 1968. He then moved on to Yale University, where he received a master of fine arts degree in 1972.

When Small found art classes that he loved, the experience changed his life. "I felt alive. I grew stronger. I knew that in this world of art I could find a place. The work never tired me. In fact, I couldn't find enough hours in the day to learn what I needed to know in order to make the kind of pictures I wanted to create."

CAREER HIGHLIGHTS

David Small is an award-winning author and illustrator of children's books. In addition to writing and illustrating six books of his own, he has served as the illustrator of many books by other well-known children's writers. As an author, Small is known for his lighthearted and humorous tales about quirky individuals who use their unique talents to gain acceptance in society. As an illustrator, his work ranges from whimsical, cartoonlike drawings to beautiful, detailed watercolors. "Small is one of the most inventive illustrators around today," Ilene Cooper wrote in *Booklist*. "His work, filled with charm and nuance, has a certain quaintness that is uniquely his own."

Becoming an Author and Illustrator

After graduating from Yale, Small decided to teach art in order to give others the education that he so desperately craved in his youth. He took jobs as a substitute teacher before landing his first full-time position as an assistant art professor at Fredonia College at State University of New York in 1972. After spending several years in New York, Small decided he wanted to move back to his home state of Michigan. In 1978, he took another position as an assistant professor of art at Kalamazoo College. He also wrote several plays during this time, but none of them were very successful.

In the late 1970s, Small began thinking about creating picture books for children. He felt that this career would enable him to combine the two

things that gave him the most pleasure—writing and drawing. He also thought that seeing his work in print would help him achieve the sense of self-satisfaction that had eluded him for years. His first book, *Eulalie and the Hopping Head,* was rejected by more than 20 publishers before it finally appeared in 1982. This book tells a strange story about a toad named Mother Lumps who finds a baby doll and thinks that it is a real human child. She adopts it in hopes that it will help teach her daughter Eulalie some manners. When the doll's head falls off, young Eulalie crawls inside and startles everyone by jumping around in it. Mother Lumps eventually decides that her daughter is perfect, despite her tendencies to misbehave.

Eulalie and the Hopping Head earned praise from critics and won several awards. For example, it was named a Parent's Choice Remarkable Book and received a citation from the Library of Congress as one of the best children's books of the year. Despite the success of his first book, however, Small still found the experience of writing and publishing it to be a tough one. "I won't say doing the book was a terrible experience, but it was grueling," he acknowledged.

"In my books I have spoken to the concerns I had as a child—those of being different from others, of being an outsider. I think of my books as a kind of dog whistle pitched high above normal human hearing, sending their signal of acceptance to the strange ones out there, telling them to hold on."

Devoting Himself to Children's Books

A short time after the publication of *Eulalie and the Hopping Head,* Small's job at Kalamazoo College was eliminated due to budget cuts. At first he considered finding another teaching position at a college, but instead he decided to use the opportunity to become a full-time professional artist and writer. He developed a humorous illustration style using such artistic media as pastel, watercolor, and pen and ink. He also started selling editorial cartoons to such publications as the *Wall Street Journal,* the *New Yorker*, and the *New York Times*.

As Small gained recognition as an artist with an original and quirky style, publishers started to approach him to illustrate works by other authors. The first book Small illustrated for another writer was Nathan Zimelman's *Mean Chickens and Wild Cucumbers*, published in 1983. Some other works to which he contributed the pictures include *The Christmas Box* and *Fighting Words* by Eve Merriman, *Petey's Bedtime Story* by Beverly Cleary, *Box and Cox* by Grace Chetwin, *The Christmas Crocodile* by Bonny Becker, and *American Politics: How it Really Works* by Milton Meltzer.

Despite his busy schedule as an illustrator, Small still managed to find the time to write and illustrate his own picture books. In each of these works, he made a commitment to develop a unique story that would stand out from other picture books. He explained that he wanted to "make a real contribution to children's literature, not simply add to the growing heap." Small decided to target his work directly at children who felt different and alone, as he had felt as a child. "In my books I have spoken to the concerns I had as a child—those of being different from others, of being an outsider," he noted. "I think of my books as a kind of dog whistle pitched high above normal human hearing, sending their signal of acceptance to the strange ones out there, telling them to hold on."

Small's second self-illustrated picture book, *Imogene's Antlers,* was published in 1985. It tells the story of a young girl named Imogene who awakens one day to find that she has grown a set of deer antlers. While her mother is horrified by the situation, Imogene embraces her uniqueness and gains acceptance by using her antlers to assist others. The next day, the antlers are gone, but Imogene has grown a peacock's tail instead. The story ends there, with the reader left to ponder how Imogene will use her new tail to her advantage. *Imogene's Antlers* was hailed for its creativity, humor, and sound message.

In 1987, Small wrote and illustrated *Paper John*. This story features a kindly man named John who lives by the sea and delights the neighboring children by constructing boats and other objects out of paper. When the devil threatens his town, it is up to John to put his talents to work and save the day. This book was another critical success for Small. Calling *Paper John* "a parable concerning the triumph of the creative imagination over the mean-spirited," a writer for *Kirkus Reviews* noted that "Small's illustrations—full of entrancing detail, including not only his cut and folded confections but a multitude of animals—are as good as he's done."

Due to his busy schedule illustrating works by other authors, it took Small five years to complete his next self-illustrated book. In 1992 he published *Ruby Mae Has Something to Say*. The title character is a woman with a speech impediment who wishes to address the United Nations about world peace but is unable to get her point across. When her nephew Billy Bob invents a wacky hat that helps her speak more clearly, Ruby Mae successfully delivers her message. A critical favorite, this book provided another example of one of Small's underdog characters overcoming their weaknesses and achieving success.

A Focus on Humor

Small's 1994 book, *George Washington's Cows,* is just plain silly. It tells the story of the absurd habits of the animals that lived on the Mount Vernon farm of the first president of the United States. The cows liked to dress up, the pigs wore wigs and threw parties, and the sheep studied literature and other scholarly pursuits. The whole thing was enough to drive Washington mad and force him to sail across the Delaware River in search of some sanity in the world of politics.

When Small collaborates on a picture book with is his wife, Sarah Stewart, they do not actually work together in the same place. "David needs a lot of space, both physically and emotionally," Stewart explained. "He plays music, loud. He's an artist. He's a guy. . . . I don't tell him what to draw. That's David's work. The only time I have a say is when David asks me. For us, that's the etiquette of the picture book. There's an enormous amount of respect between us for each other's work."

Small pushed the level of absurdity even further in his 1995 book, *Hoover's Bride*. The main character, Hoover, is an eccentric and sloppy man who lives in a filthy house. One day he gets a vacuum cleaner that he uses successfully to clean the place. Hoover is so impressed by the appliance that he falls in love with it and proposes marriage. The odd couple's honeymoon is cut short when the vacuum runs away with a lawnmower that was recently wed to a woman. Hoover and the woman then fall in love and decide to get married. Meanwhile, their mechanical former spouses end up in the city dump without any gas or electricity to make them go.

In 1996, Small published another book that features a lonely soul in search of acceptance. *Fenwick's Suit* tells the story of an unpopular man who does not have any friends at work. When he passes a store with a flashy suit in its window, Fenwick purchases the suit on the spot, in hopes that it will help liven up his dreary life. His plan works, and Fenwick is soon one of the most popular fellows in the office. But he eventually realizes that it is the suit that his co-workers are attracted to, not him. Fenwick decides to get rid of the suit, only to discover that it has gained a mind of its own and has no desire to be disposed of. The book concludes with Fenwick and his suit facing off in a memorable and zany showdown.

Collaborating with His Wife

By writing and illustrating his own stories, Small was finally able to happily live out his dream. "Of all the things I do now as an artist, the creation of children's books is the most pleasurable," he said. But Small also enjoyed illustrating the work of other authors, and the results were quite successful.

Small's favorite author to work with is his wife, Sarah Stewart. When the couple collaborates on a picture book, however, they do not actually work together in the same place. Stewart writes in a quiet room in their small home, while Small produces the pictures in an 1890s Victorian farmhouse on their property. His studio includes books, a collection of pencils, brushes, paints, papers, and other art supplies, and a small gym setup with weight-lifting equipment. "David needs a lot of space, both physically and emotionally," Stewart explained. "He plays music, loud. He's an artist. He's a guy." Stewart likes to give Small a lot of freedom when he is illustrating one of her stories. "I don't tell him what to draw," she stated. "That's David's work. The only time I have a say is when David asks me. For us, that's the etiquette of the picture book. There's an enormous amount of respect between us for each other's work," she continued.

Small and Stewart's first book together, *The Money Tree,* was published in 1991. It tells the story of a woman who finds a tree growing in her yard that sprouts dollar bills instead of leaves. All summer long, she watches through the window as her friends and neighbors greedily pick money from the tree. As winter approaches, she decides to cut down the tree and use it for firewood to keep her house warm. "Though its message may be beyond the reach of some readers, Stewart's first book will raise worthwhile questions for both children and adults," wrote a reviewer for *Publishers Weekly*. "Yet more exceptional than the story are Small's paintings."

The couple's 1996 book, *The Gardener,* was their most successful joint effort to date. It tells a simple story about a young girl named Lydia Grace who brings joy to others through her love of gardening. The tenderness of this

tale allowed Small to break away from his usual whimsical, cartoonlike illustration style and create drawings that were a bit softer. This move paid off in 1998, when the American Library Association named *The Gardener* as a runner-up for the Caldecott Medal, the highest award given to illustrators of children's books.

Small joined with his wife once again to produce *The Journey,* which was published in 2001. It tells the tale of a young Amish girl who visits Chicago for the first time and records her experiences in her diary. This gentle story about the joys of home earned the husband-and-wife team further critical acclaim. As Wendy Lukeheart wrote in *School Library Journal,* "This title offers so much: a glimpse into Amish culture and Chicago treasures; a winsome main character and many sensitively depicted supporting personalities; a fresh, authentic voice; and a design perfectly melded to its simple message."

Winning the Caldecott Medal

In 2000, Small collaborated with author Judith St. George on a book entitled *So You Want to Be President?* This work is a collection of fun facts and trivia about the first 41 men who have held the top office in the United States. Small was able to draw on his experience as a political cartoonist to create a series of memorable and often humorous caricatures of all the American presidents. Small's drawings of Abraham Lincoln, William Howard Taft, Bill Clinton, Richard Nixon, Ronald Reagan, Thomas Jefferson, and George Washington were among the most memorable in the book.

Small poured his heart and soul into the assignment and spent many hours at the library looking at photos and official paintings of the presidents in order to get their looks exactly the way he wanted. He opted for his traditional humorous approach instead of a more realistic style. "Although the subjects took a tremendous amount of serious research, humor is the only way I could approach this book," he recalled. "Not only is humor my style, it certainly is the only approach that seems appropriate for politics." The result was an educational and fun-to-read book about the good and bad things that come with living in the White House.

So You Want to Be President? was a rousing success and earned Small the coveted Caldecott Medal. Small was ecstatic when he found out that he won the highest honor for picture book illustrators. It was a cold Michigan winter morning when he received a phone call giving him the news. "I was standing in my pajamas, making coffee, feeling sorry for myself. Then the phone rang and suddenly the sun came up!" Small remembered. "It's a wonderful honor, the highest in the field. I don't know what the Caldecott will do to my life, but I'm sure it will turn me around in some way." Winning the Caldecott Honor for *The Gardener* was very special for Small, but claiming the Caldecott Medal for *So You Want to Be President?* was even more satisfying. "Comparing the Caldecotts to the Olympics, the Honor is the silver and the Medal is the gold," he explained.

"

Small was ecstatic when he found out that his book So You Want to Be President? *had won the Caldecott Medal. It was a cold Michigan winter morning when he received a phone call giving him the news. "I was standing in my pajamas, making coffee, feeling sorry for myself. Then the phone rang and suddenly the sun came up! It's a wonderful honor, the highest in the field. I don't know what the Caldecott will do to my life, but I'm sure it will turn me around in some way."*

"

In June 2001, in giving an acceptance speech for the Caldecott, Small gave credit to the two men who were running for president at the time for helping his book achieve a bit more attention. "I want to send thanks to George W. Bush and Al Gore for prolonging the election so that our book could stay on the *New York Times* best-seller list for a few extra weeks. Nice work, fellas!" he said.

On a more serious note in his acceptance speech, Small also spoke about the importance of art, music, dance, and drama in children's lives and in school curriculum. He related some of the experiences he and his wife, Sarah, had had while visiting schools around the country. "In all our travels this spring, to schools and libraries in cities from one coast to another, Sarah and I have been disturbed more than ever before by the nearly total

eradication of the arts from the schools in America. Children who need the expressive outlet of art, music, dance, and playacting have none of it. At the best they listen to a visiting author or artist for 45 minutes, and those people might as well be visiting from the moon, so remote are most children from the real, human, and very necessary activities of writing, of drawing, of playing an instrument. These things are deemed by school administrators as luxuries when they are in fact necessities. As someone so rightly pointed out, few people get chills from doing a math problem. Art and music are the things which speak to the human soul. These necessary tools of human expression have become the exclusive property of a small elite group when they should be readily available to all American schoolchildren. . . .

"We have seen flourishing arts programs in a few schools. There the hallways and classrooms are richly covered with paintings and filled with music, making these environments quite simply delightful to be in, as well as a delight to learn in. But these are for the most part in private schools in wealthy communities. But even wealth is not an indicator of a full education for the children. In March, while on a book-tour, Sarah and I were in emerging affluent neighborhoods with new elementary schools where there were no arts programs and the libraries had been lost to computer centers. In all too many schools across America, the halls are silent and the walls are empty but for a list of rules to follow in case of a fire drill. (When I see a wall full of colored-in xeroxed turkeys I also see emptiness. I am also underwhelmed when I listen to anyone extolling the virtues of the computer over things created by hand, as if drawing, painting, and sculpture are activities related to the Pliocene epoch.)"

Small told one group of students during a school visit: "You will have a happy life if you do what you love. And the other thing is, if you have someone at home who loves you, you will have a completely happy life."

Small's Writing Philosophy

Small is thrilled that he has been able to earn a living doing the two things that he most enjoys—writing and drawing. Still, he stresses that writing and illustrating books is hard work and takes a great deal of dedication. "It takes months and months to get a book into shape," he noted. "A children's book takes one or two years, to write the text and research and illustrate it. Sometimes it goes smoothly, and sometimes not." Small also feels that coming up with an idea is actually more difficult than writing a story about it. "Once I get an idea, I don't have any problem writing it. But a new idea is very hard to come up with," he said. "A new twist on something is not that easy."

Small likes visiting with children and discussing his books with them. As Small told one group of students during a school visit: "You will have a happy life if you do what you love. And the other thing is, if you have someone at home who loves you, you will have a completely happy life."

MARRIAGE AND FAMILY

David Small married Sarah Stewart in 1980. They met in New York, when they were both teaching college. It was the second marriage for them both. They have five grown children between them—two from Small's first marriage, and three from Stewart's. The couple lives in an old Greek Revival house in rural Mendon, Michigan. When they are not creating books, they enjoy gardening and other aspects of the quiet life.

SELECTED WORKS

As Author and Illustrator

Eulalie and the Hopping Head, 1982
Imogene's Antlers, 1985
Paper John, 1987
Ruby Mae Has Something to Say, 1992
George Washington's Cows, 1994
Fenwick's Suit, 1996

As Illustrator

Mean Chickens and Wild Cucumbers, 1983 (written by Nathan Zimelman)
Gulliver's Travels, 1983 (written by Jonathan Swift)
Anna and the Seven Swans, 1984 (written by Maida Silverman)
The Kuklapolitan Players Present: The Dragon Who Lived Downstairs, 1984 (written by Burr Tillstrom)
The Christmas Box, 1985 (written by Eve Merriman)
Company's Coming, 1988 (written by Arthur Yorinks)
The King Has Horse's Ears, 1988 (written by Peggy Thomson)
American Politics: How it Really Works, 1989 (written by Milton Meltzer)
As: A Surfeit of Similes, 1989 (written by Norton Juster)
Box and Cox, 1990 (written by Grace Chetwin)
The Money Tree, 1991 (written by Sarah Stewart)
Fighting Words, 1992 (written by Eve Merriman)
Petey's Bedtime Story, 1993 (written by Beverly Cleary)
The Library, 1995 (written by Sarah Stewart)
The Gardener, 1996 (written by Sarah Stewart)
The Huckabuck Family and How They Raised Popcorn in Nebraska and Quit and Came Back, 1996 (written by Carl Sandburg)
The Christmas Crocodile, 1998 (written by Bonny Becker)
As Silly As Knees, As Busy As Bees: An Astounding Assortment of Similes, 1998 (written by Norton Juster)

So You Want to Be President? 2000 (written by Judith St. George)
The Journey, 2001 (written by Sarah Stewart)
Mouse and His Child, 2001 (written by Russell Hoban)

HONORS AND AWARDS

Children's Book of the Year List (Library of Congress): 1982, for *Eulalie and the Hopping Head*
Parents' Choice Remarkable Book (Parents' Choice Foundation): 1982, for *Eulalie and the Hopping Head*
Notable Book for Children in the Field of Social Studies (National Council of Social Studies): 1983, for *Mean Chickens and Wild Cucumbers*
Children's Books of the Year List (Child Study Association of America): 1985, for *The Christmas Box*
Parents' Choice Award for Literature (Parents' Choice Foundation): 1985, for *Imogene's Antlers*
Redbook Award (American Library Association): 1988, for *Company's Coming*
Parents' Choice Award for Picture Books (Parents' Choice Foundation): 1989, for *As: A Surfeit of Similes*; 1990, for *Box and Cox*
Randolph Caldecott Medal (American Library Association): 2001, for *So You Want to Be President?*

FURTHER READING

Books

Contemporary Authors New Revision Series, Vol. 39
Holtze, Sally Holmes, ed. *Sixth Book of Junior Authors & Illustrators*, 1989
Something About the Author, Vol. 95, 1998

Periodicals

Austin American-Statesman, Sep. 22, 1996, p.G6
Booklist, June 15, 1987, p.1608
Boston Globe, Jan. 21, 2001, p.F5
Detroit Free Press, Oct. 22, 1982, p.C9; Jan. 16, 2001, p.A1
Detroit News, Jan. 16, 2001
Horn Book, July/Aug. 2001, p.411
Kansas City (Mo.) Star, Sep. 28, 1999, p.E1
Kirkus Reviews, Apr. 15, 1987, p.643
New York Times, Sep. 17, 2000, p.32; Jan. 16, 2001, p. E9; May 20, 2001, p.32
Pittsburgh Post Gazette, Jan. 16, 2001, p.B1

Publishers Weekly, Aug. 30, 1991, p.83
School Library Journal, Nov. 2000, p.42; Mar. 2001, p.220
South Bend (Ind.) Tribune, Mar. 22, 1996, p.C1
U.S. News and World Report, Aug. 7, 2000, p.78; Jan. 29, 2001, p.8

ADDRESS

Farrar, Straus & Giroux
19 Union Square West
New York, NY 10013

WORLD WIDE WEB SITE

http://www.nccil.org/exhibits

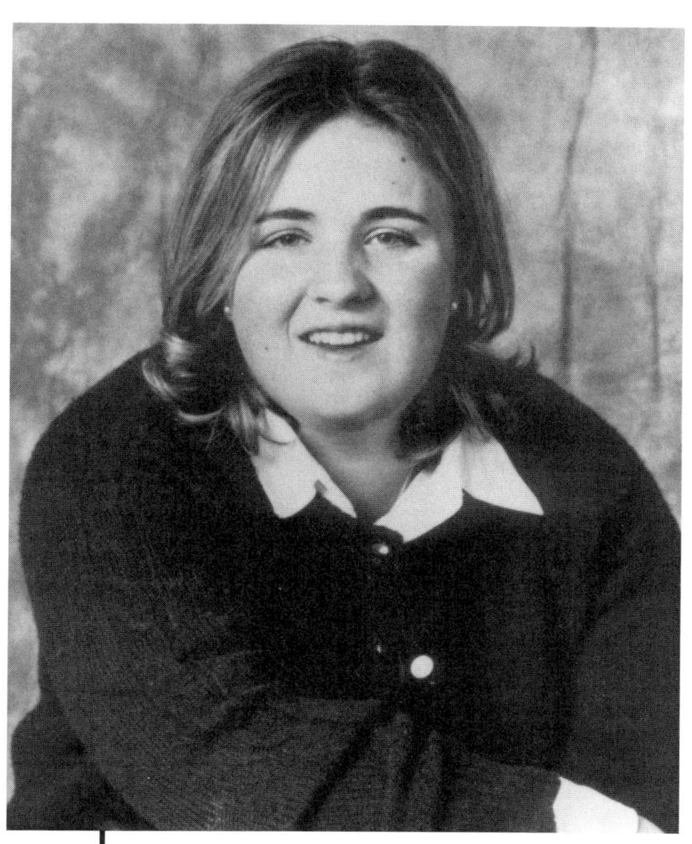

Katie Tarbox 1982-

American College Student and Writer
Author of *Katie.com,* a True Story about the Dangers of the Internet

BIRTH

Katherine Tarbox, better known as Katie, was born on January 26, 1982, in New Canaan, Connecticut. Her mother, Andrea Tarbox, works as a financial officer at a computer company. Her biological father left the family shortly after she was born. When Katie was four, her mother married David Gransee, a pharmaceutical company executive. She has an older sister, Abby, and a younger half-sister, Carrie.

YOUTH

From the outside, Tarbox's life in the wealthy suburb of New Canaan seemed perfect. The family was financially well-to-do. They lived in a large home with a nanny and a housekeeper. Katie had a huge wardrobe of nice clothes. She was an excellent student and a member of a nationally ranked swim team. She even had a personal trainer to help her prepare for swim meets. But underneath, Tarbox felt lonely and insecure. "Home was a place where I always felt alone," she stated.

Tarbox's mother worked long hours and was rarely home. While she admired her mother for being successful and supporting the family, she wished that they could spend more time together. Tarbox also struggled to develop a relationship with her stepfather. "I have always held a certain image of an ideal father in my head," she explained in *Katie.com*, her memoir about her teenage experiences. "It's based on what I heard about my friend's fathers. They took their daughters to baseball games, gave them clothes they wouldn't ordinarily get when they went shopping, and served them sugar for breakfast. David didn't do any of this, and whenever I asked him anything, the reply was, 'Go ask your mother.' After a while I just stopped asking him. Going to David was a waste of time. This is why I have never considered David my father."

Like many teenagers, Tarbox spent a lot of time worrying about her appearance and whether she fit in with her peers. She became obsessed with fashion magazines and tried never to wear the same outfit twice in a month. In her mind, it seemed like everyone she met in her upper-middle-class town was slender and had perfect teeth. As a result, she felt insecure about her body. "At 13, I accepted the image of beauty I saw on the covers of fashion magazines. I thought the Calvin Klein models inside were beautiful. I thought ultra-thinness was beautiful. Beauty was painful. And it was very expensive," she wrote in her book. "I hated my legs then, just as much as I do now. At 13 I already had the biggest thighs in the world. They were so huge that my mom wouldn't even buy me a skirt that was above the knee."

Looking for Friends in Internet Chat Rooms

In 1995, at the age of 13, Tarbox used her older sister's laptop computer to access the Internet. Bored and lonely, she spent a couple of hours each day online. She spent most of this time in Internet chat rooms trying to meet other teenagers who shared her interests. At this point, Tarbox had never had a boyfriend and felt alienated from classmates who were sexually active. So she was surprised and a little disgusted to find that sex was a huge topic of discussion in teen-oriented chat rooms. "Entering a chat room is like entering a party where you don't know anyone. You start by telling everyone the same thing over and over again: the basics about age, gender, location, interests," she explained. "Inevitably things get around to sex and appearance. All the guys online say they are at least six feet tall with brown hair and blue eyes. They all describe themselves as if they are Tom Cruise's taller twin. And they all want to know what you look like, especially your body. You can be sure that every time you go online someone is going to ask you your breast size. I don't really see why anyone bothers to ask. Everyone lies when they answer."

"Entering a chat room is like entering a party where you don't know anyone. You start by telling everyone the same thing over and over again: the basics about age, gender, location, interests. Inevitably things get around to sex and appearance. All the guys online say they are at least six feet tall with brown hair and blue eyes. They all describe themselves as if they are Tom Cruise's taller twin. And they all want to know what you look like, especially your body. You can be sure that every time you go online someone is going to ask you your breast size. I don't really see why anyone bothers to ask. Everyone lies when they answer."

Even though she felt uncomfortable with the emphasis on sex, Tarbox continued to enter chat rooms in hopes of making a real connection with someone. "Despite all of the weirdos and the creepy feeling of being detached from reality," she noted, "a small part of me believed that there was someone out there on the Web like me. I knew this person wouldn't be easy to find, and he wasn't. Every time I met someone we'd exchange basic data and then search around for something real to discuss, but I would slowly realize we had very little at all in common."

Tarbox eventually found the person she had been looking for—a man who said his name was Mark. Mark claimed that he was a 23-year-old college student from California. He seemed to share every interest that Tarbox mentioned. "I was excited that I had met someone just like me, but of the opposite sex. He even liked Mozart! At last I had connected with another kind, intelligent soul. Best of all, he recognized me as someone different from the typical 13-year-old," she recalled. "I was impressed by the fact that he typed with proper punctuation and capitalized proper nouns and the first word of his sentences. Excellent grammar. A good vocabulary. I thought he *must* be all right."

While Tarbox was initially concerned about the 10-year difference in their ages, she was soon overcome by Mark's charm. He told the insecure girl that she was smart, funny, mature, and sophisticated. In her loneliness, he made her feel loved and appreciated. "I guess I was naive," she admitted. "I always longed for adult attention —most teenage girls love it when an older guy takes an interest. And I wasn't street smart. I was used to trusting adults. It didn't occur to me that they might lie to me." Within a month, Tarbox and her online friend had exchanged phone numbers. They spoke on the phone often, usually in the middle of the night when her parents were asleep. Over time, Mark gradually alienated Tarbox from her friends and family. He made it seem as if he was the only one who cared about her and understood her problems.

"I was excited that I had met someone just like me, but of the opposite sex. He even liked Mozart! At last I had connected with another kind, intelligent soul. Best of all, he recognized me as someone different from the typical 13-year-old. I was impressed by the fact that he typed with proper punctuation and capitalized proper nouns and the first word of his sentences. Excellent grammar. A good vocabulary. I thought he must *be all right."*

Agreeing to Meet Her Online Friend

After six months of exchanging e-mail and phone calls with Mark, Tarbox agreed to meet him face to face. She told him that she would be traveling with her swim team to a national meet in Houston, Texas, and he arranged to get a room at the same hotel. Tarbox's mother accompanied the team to Houston as a chaperone, but she was unaware of her daughter's online relationship or the planned meeting. On the night of March 12, 1996, Andrea Tarbox left the hotel to buy bagels for breakfast the next morning. At this point, Katie went to see Mark in his hotel room. Luckily, she told one of her teammates where she was going.

Tarbox was excited finally to meet Mark. She felt so certain of their relationship that she did not even bother getting dressed up to see him. Instead, she went to his room wearing her pajamas. "I was excited. I was

going to see someone who I felt was very special to me," she remembered. "It did not enter my head that he would want sex with me. I was only 13 and not interested in that type of thing. He was my friend and I was going to see my friend for the first time."

When Mark opened the door, however, it was clear that he had lied about his age and appearance. Upon seeing a much-older man, Tarbox began to feel some doubts for the first time. "This wasn't at all what I had expected," she noted. "We were such good friends—more than friends—on the Internet. No one had ever made me feel safer and more at ease. But here, in his presence, I was anxious and confused." But Tarbox overcame her fears and entered Mark's room.

Within a few minutes, Mark began kissing her and putting his hands inside her shirt and pants. Tarbox was so shocked by his behavior that she froze. "Instead of being angry and shouting at him to stop it, I was confused and speechless," she remembered. "Mark was supposed to be better than this. He was supposed to be patient and kind and generous. He was supposed to care about me. Now it was clear that he obviously wanted me to have sex with him. That was what this meeting was about."

At that moment, someone began pounding on the door of the hotel room. "The knocking on the door was so loud that it made me panic," Tarbox recalled. "I have never been so instantly frightened. It sounded as if a giant were pounding on the door." Andrea Tarbox had returned from buying bagels and gone to kiss her daughter goodnight. When Katie was not in her room, she convinced her teammate to tell her what had happened. Andrea Tarbox then rushed to Mark's room, bringing two swim coaches and hotel security with her. They arrived just in time to stop a possible rape.

"Instead of being angry and shouting at him to stop it, I was confused and speechless. Mark was supposed to be better than this. He was supposed to be patient and kind and generous. He was supposed to care about me. Now it was clear that he obviously wanted me to have sex with him. That was what this meeting was about."

Becoming Involved in a Sexual Molestation Case

Shortly after being rescued from the hotel room, Tarbox learned that Mark was not who he had pretended to be. The man she met was actually Frank Kufrovich, a 41-year-old financial consultant with a history of sexually molesting children. He had made several trips to Asia—where some teenagers and pre-teens work as prostitutes—in order to have sex with children. He had also formed relationships with both girls and boys online for the purpose of meeting them for sex.

Even when she learned the truth about her Internet friend, however, Tarbox felt obligated to protect him. At first, she followed Kufrovich's instructions and told her mother and the police that nothing had happened between them in the hotel room. She struggled to understand how Mark—who had seemed truly to care about her—and Frank could be the same person. Over time, however, Tarbox realized that she had to admit the truth. "Gradually, the man who had been my friend, who had listened to me and cared for me so deeply, was fading from view," she noted. "He was being replaced by the image of a manipulative, porn-obsessed, child molester named Frank Kufrovich. This was not my Mark. But he was the one who had created Mark."

After wrestling with her feelings for a week, Tarbox finally told her mother that Kufrovich had molested her. Andrea Tarbox was disappointed that Katie had lied and used poor judgment, but she helped her daughter find the courage to press charges against him. Kufrovich thus became the first person to be prosecuted under the 1996 Communications Decency Act as an Internet child molester. Unfortunately, the legal case took two years and created great hardships for Tarbox. First, Kufrovich denied the charges and demanded that she take a lie-detector test. Then he claimed that Tarbox was a stalker who would not leave him alone. He even sent private detectives to her school to try to find evidence that she was promiscuous. Tarbox had to relate her story in dozens of police interviews and testify in front of a grand jury. Finally, in 1998, Kufrovich reached an agreement with the prosecutors. He pleaded guilty to various charges and was sentenced to 18 months in prison. "It was a very long legal process, and it drained a lot out of me," Tarbox admitted. "It was the hardest part of my life. But there was no way we were going to let this thing go."

Even though the legal battle was hard for Tarbox, the most difficult part of her experience was coping with the reactions of her family and friends. People she trusted treated her really badly afterward. Although Tarbox was the victim, everyone unfairly blamed her. "When you think about what had happened in that hotel room, it was not as big a deal as everything that happened afterward," she noted. "The way everyone — my family, the swim team, school friends, teachers — had reacted had made it much worse. And while they were all saying that they were upset about what had happened to me, no one seemed very interested in accepting me or comforting me. Instead they talked about how I was responsible, how I had let everyone down, disgraced myself, behaved terribly. It almost seemed like they were saying I got what I deserved."

"When you think about what had happened in that hotel room, it was not as big a deal as everything that happened afterward. The way everyone — my family, the swim team, school friends, teachers — had reacted had made it much worse. And while they were all saying that they were upset about what had happened to me, no one seemed very interested in accepting me or comforting me. Instead they talked about how I was responsible, how I had let everyone down, disgraced myself, behaved terribly. It almost seemed like they were saying I got what I deserved."

Immediately after the incident in the hotel room, Tarbox's coaches made her apologize to the swim team for causing them to lose their concentration just before the national meet. When she returned to school, her classmates spread terrible rumors about her. When her older sister heard what had happened, she told Katie, "I'm really disgusted with you. You've ruined our family. You've ruined our lives." Even though Tarbox was the victim of a sexual predator, few people gave her compassion or support. She lost all of her friends and ended up feeling guilty and confused. "Very few of my old friends wanted to associate with me, and even those who may have wanted to felt they couldn't," she noted. "Their parents wouldn't allow it. To them I wasn't the victim of a crime who deserved compassion. I had been stupid, or maybe seductive, and placed myself in danger. I was a bad influence."

"Very few of my old friends wanted to associate with me, and even those who may have wanted to felt they couldn't. Their parents wouldn't allow it. To them I wasn't the victim of a crime who deserved compassion. I had been stupid, or maybe seductive, and placed myself in danger. I was a bad influence."

”

EDUCATION

Tarbox was an excellent student throughout her school years in New Canaan. At New Canaan High School, she participated in choir, played the piano, and was a member of a nationally ranked swim team. But once her fellow students learned that she had been molested by a man she had met over the Internet, Tarbox felt that she could not attend the school any longer. She transferred to St. Paul's School, an exclusive boarding school in New Hampshire, in 1998. "It gave me a clean start," she commented. After graduating from St. Paul's with honors in 2000, Tarbox went on to the University of Pennsylvania. As she completed her freshman year in 2001, she was majoring in English and considering going to law school.

BECOMING A WRITER

Writing a Book about Her Experience

In the two years between when she was molested in the hotel room and when Kufrovich was sentenced, Tarbox struggled to deal with her feelings of guilt and shame over what had happened. "For two years, I actually thought I was guilty for it," she stated. "I viewed it as me sending him to jail. It took me a long time to realize that I was just 13. That's a very naive age. It took me a while to realize that a 13-year-old can't be responsible for a sexual encounter with a 41-year-old man." Tarbox hit her emotional low point during the summer of 1998. One day, without really realizing what she was doing, she climbed into the shower fully dressed and sat there crying uncontrollably under the running water. Her family then decided that she needed more intensive therapy than she had received so far.

As a way to deal with the emotional impact of her experience, Tarbox began writing about it. "Right after [Kufrovich] was sentenced, I didn't feel healed," she explained. "I didn't feel like it was over. I turned to writing to deal with these things." Throughout the summer, she spent hours each day turning her anger and guilt into words on her computer screen. "I wasn't eating, I wasn't showering," she recalled. "All I wanted to do was write." Tarbox never really expected to write a book, but by the end of the summer her manuscript was 300 pages long. She found a literary agent to represent her, and before long five major publishing houses were competing over the rights to publish her story. The book, *Katie.com: My Story*, was published by Dutton in 2000.

Why Tarbox Wrote the Book

While Tarbox knew it would be difficult to let strangers read about what had happened to her, she felt that publishing the book might help other people avoid a similar situation. "Part of my decision to write this book was because this case was so emotionally draining," she explained. "[Kufrovich] did this to many girls, and a few boys. After he was sentenced, all I could think was, 'What if one of those girls had come forward?' I would have been saved. So I came forward. So I was willing to take some risks." In addition, the process of writing and publishing the book helped Tarbox overcome her feelings of shame about being the victim of molestation. "Writing the book, and having to come to terms with all of this, I no longer feel ashamed," she stated. "I've taken this situation in my life and turned it around into something positive."

One of Tarbox's goals in publishing her book was to educate people about sex crimes against children. "When I was going through all this, the court and the trial, I was surrounded by walls of ignorance on Internet pedophilia," she noted. "It was time to get a clear message across about molestation and rape, so that maybe some other girls can be saved from this. The way we treat molestation and rape victims in this country is absolutely embarrassing. This is a very real part of our society. The more I learn, the more

cases I hear about where a sexual crime has occurred and people don't come forward. They don't prosecute. I understand this is a very shameful thing. The more we silently accept it, the more it continues."

Tarbox also hoped that her book would help people understand that anyone could become a victim. "Really, my book is about trying to grow up in a very confusing society," she explained. "People in New Canaan think that nothing bad can happen to you if you're rich. Before this happened, I'd never have believed I could be a victim of molestation. I thought a girl had to be promiscuous for this to happen. . . . It was better for [the people of New Canaan] to think I was someone really bad; otherwise they had to face the possibility that it could have happened to them, too. We like to stereotype victims to distance ourselves from them."

Tarbox does not present her family life in a positive light in her book. She says that her parents did not spend enough time developing a close relationship with her or monitoring her activities online. "I didn't want to cover anything up, or sugarcoat it," she stated. "If people thought we had a 'Brady Bunch' existence, no one would have been able to understand how this happened. Our relationships were at an all-time low and it made me turn to other things. I can't stress enough, though, that although I thought my family relationships were bad, they were not unique." Despite the criticism, however, Andrea Tarbox was very supportive of Katie's efforts to write and publish her story.

Reaction to *Katie.com*

When *Katie.com* was published, it received many positive reviews and became a best-seller. "Strong, articulate, and conservative, Tarbox evokes pity and admiration with her heartfelt account of a precocious girl who was deceived and then betrayed," said a *Publishers Weekly* reviewer. Writing in *Time,* Anita Hamilton called the book "an impressive work that reveals not just the danger of online pedophilia but also the tormented psyche of a young teen who seemed to have it all." Michelle Malkin of *Insight on the News* added that "this true-life horror story should be required reading for parents in the Internet age."

Unfortunately, the publication of Tarbox's book also created some controversy. The title her publisher chose for the book, *Katie.com,* was an actual Internet domain name that belonged to a businesswoman from London, England. Katie Jones, the owner of a computer company that hosted a popular online discussion group, had used the domain name for her personal Web site since 1996. When the book was published under that name, Jones received 100,000 e-mails that were intended for Tarbox. She was very angry that the publisher had used the name without her permission. But Dutton refused to take any action to correct the situation. "Yes there's freedom of speech, but not absolute freedom. To effectively print a book with someone's address on it goes too far," Jones said. "I can't see any reason for calling the book after a domain name that they don't own, because they're sending traffic to me instead of to them, which is silly. They're not getting the full benefit of it."

"I think if teens read this book, and understand that they're at risk, and learn to use the Internet in a safe way, and don't start these relationships, then that's what I really hope for," Tarbox said. "I do not go into chat rooms anymore. I do use the Internet in other ways, and I think it's a great tool. But I don't think it's a safe way to meet people."

The Dangers of the Internet

Tarbox spent the summer before she started college traveling around the United States on a promotional book tour. She gave interviews for magazines and newspapers, participated in Internet chats, and appeared on several television news programs. Tarbox used the publicity surrounding her book to raise public awareness of the dangers of Internet predators. Studies show that one out of five American teenagers using the Internet have been propositioned for sex by strangers. The Federal Bureau of Investigation (FBI) set up a special program called Innocent Images to catch pedophiles operating over the Internet. FBI agents enter chat rooms posing as 13- and 14-year-olds and then arrest people who pursue them for sex. The program led to the arrest of 500 people between 1995 and 1999.

Internet Safety Tips

The Internet is a wonderful tool for finding information and even for connecting with people. But it can also be dangerous if it's used unwisely. Remember that when you're online in a chat room or in a newsgroup, you're in a public forum where anyone can read what you post. Don't post anything that you don't want read by the general public. Also, because all postings are anonymous, it's impossible to tell who you are communicating with. Most people will be exactly who they say they are. But people on the Internet can pretend to be anyone they want, so you have to protect yourself against predators. Have fun and stay safe!

- **Do not give out any personal information that could be used to figure out your identity.**
  That includes your name, address, city, and phone number. Also, don't give out your school name, sports teams' names, where you take dance or gymnastic classes, where you hang out after school and on the weekend, or similar types of information about your regular activities. And do not give out any of these types of information about your family or friends. If anyone asks for personal information, don't tell them.

- **Never get together with someone you've met online.**
  You can't be sure the person is really who they say they are. If you ever do think about meeting someone, do it only with your parents' permission. Plan to meet in a public place that you are familiar with and have your parents accompany you to the meeting. Never go alone.

- **Don't talk on the phone to anyone you've met online.**

- **Don't use any part of your real name in your screen name.**
  Make up a fun name to use online so that you can't be identified. Pick a gender-neutral name so your sex can't be determined.

- **Never show your picture to anyone online.**
  Letting someone know what you look like could help them identify you.

- **Be careful about what information you put into a profile with your online service provider.**
  Your personal profile will be read by other people online. Make sure you don't put any personal identifying information there.

- **Protect your privacy.**
  Web sites will sometimes ask for information about you. They can then share that information with other groups or businesses without your permission. Never enter any personal information without first checking with your parents.

- **Don't respond to email, chat room comments, or newsgroup postings that are hostile or that make you feel uncomfortable.**
  If you get a message like that, simply don't respond. Don't get into arguments online. Show the offensive material to your parents or another adult you trust.

- **If something seems wrong, hostile, offensive, or inappropriate, it probably is. Get help.**

- **If you're having problems with someone online, get help.**
  Talk to an adult you trust. You could talk to your parents, a teacher, or your counselor at school. Show them the message that's bothering you and ask for their help.

- **Here are some web sites you can visit for further information on keeping safe on the Internet:**
  http://www.safeteens.com
  http://www.cyberangels.com
  http://www.wiredteens.org
  http://www.ftc.gov/bcp/conline/edcams/kidzprivacy/index.html

In many of her interviews, Tarbox was asked to provide fellow teenagers with tips for navigating the Internet safely. She tells kids never to give out personal information online, including their hometown or school; never to agree to see someone they have met online; and always to be skeptical about what people say in Internet chat rooms. "I think if teens read this book, and understand that they're at risk, and learn to use the Internet in a

Some of Katie's family (from left): her sister, Abby; her stepfather, David; Katie; and her mother, Andrea.

safe way, and don't start these relationships, then that's what I really hope for," she stated. "I do not go into chat rooms anymore. I do use the Internet in other ways, and I think it's a great tool. But I don't think it's a safe way to meet people."

Tarbox also recommends that parents take steps to prevent their children from corresponding with possible pedophiles online. These steps include informing kids about the potential dangers lurking online; putting the home computer in a high-traffic area rather than in a child's bedroom; and using filtering software or subscribing to a children-oriented online service. Tarbox also feels that it is important for parents to make time for their kids, listen to their problems, and help them set goals so that they will be less likely to become victims. "Too many girls seem willing to believe that their worth is determined by other people," she explained. "The Internet has created a new avenue for the predators who would exploit this insecurity. Girls who have goals, real connections to family and friends, and a sense that a world of opportunity awaits them seem to be inoculated against this danger."

Finally, Tarbox tells parents to watch for warning signs that their children may be involved with an Internet predator, such as spending a lot of time online, especially at night; hiding the computer monitor from view when another person enters the room; receiving phone calls from a stranger or making calls to an unknown number; receiving gifts or packages from a stranger; or withdrawing from the family.

Following the success of her book, Tarbox set up a Web site called www.KatieT.com to help educate parents and teens about the dangers lurking in cyberspace. She has received thousands of e-mails from people who read her book. Many of these notes express support and appreciation for her bravery in coming forward. Other notes come from teenagers who want to share their own stories of sexual molestation. But she also receives e-mail messages from people who say that she got what she deserved for agreeing to meet a stranger in a hotel room. Tarbox leaves these notes on her Web site so that readers can see how some people blame the victim in cases of sexual assault. "I think a lot of people start to understand what a victim goes through when they read this," she stated. "If I can give people that understanding, then I'm happy to do it. I think it's made the supporters a lot stronger."

"I have learned how to be tenacious through the judicial system. I have learned that life is not fair. I have learned to believe in myself. I have learned that how a person handles setbacks really speaks a lot about their character. I have learned that nothing good in life should be taken for granted. I am now trying to take the most horrible situation in my life and turn it into the most positive aspect in my life. And I believe that this represents a great accomplishment."

As the final step in her healing process, Tarbox gave a speech about her experience in front of 600 classmates and teachers at St. Paul's School. "I needed to do something public, something that would destroy all the secrecy and maybe, in the process, lift my shame. The shame would only go away when the truth was told and accepted by everyone who was important to me," she noted. She told the students about some of the lessons she had learned. "I have learned how to be tenacious through the judicial system. I have learned that life is not fair. I have learned to believe in my-

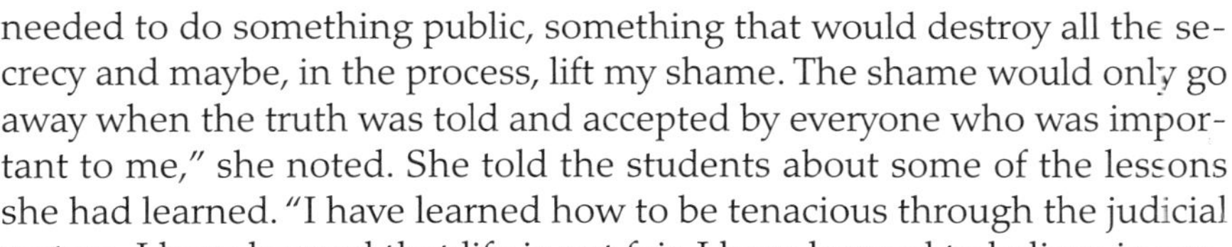

self. I have learned that how a person handles setbacks really speaks a lot about their character. I have learned that nothing good in life should be taken for granted," she said. "I am now trying to take the most horrible situation in my life and turn it into the most positive aspect in my life. And I believe that this represents a great accomplishment." Upon receiving a standing ovation, Tarbox realized that "finally, I was no longer a victim."

HOME AND FAMILY

Since the incident in the hotel room and the publication of her book, Tarbox has grown closer to her family. "Obviously, this incident was a big wake-up call for my family," she noted. "It made us look at our relationships. It took a lot of work and a lot of time, but I am happy to say I have a very close relationship with my mother, a better one with my stepfather, and my older and younger sisters and I are close."

"Obviously, this incident was a big wake-up call for my family. It made us look at our relationships. It took a lot of work and a lot of time, but I am happy to say I have a very close relationship with my mother, a better one with my stepfather, and my older and younger sisters and I are close."

Tarbox believes that she has recovered from her ordeal enough to begin dating. She hopes to get married and have a family someday. "It's going to take a very strong guy, because I've made a little bit of money and there's a lot of publicity and guys are a little intimidated. I haven't found that guy yet," she stated. "I think right now I'm ready to start dating and be in a relationship. I'll have to see. I'll have to take it one day at a time."

HOBBIES AND OTHER INTERESTS

During her time off from college, Tarbox is working on a book about the college application process. She is basing her second work on her own experience of applying to 17 schools and only being accepted into one.

WRITINGS

Katie.com: My Story, 2000

FURTHER READING

Books

Tarbox, Katherine. *Katie.com: My Story,* 2000

Periodicals

Daily Telegraph (London), July 4, 2000, p.17
Dallas Morning News, May 21, 2000, p.F1
Guardian (London), Aug. 7, 2000, p.46
Hartford (Conn.) Courant, May 1, 2000, p.D2
Houston Chronicle, May 7, 2000, Lifestyle sec., p.1
New York Post, May 10, 2000, p.8
People, May 29, 2000, p.95
Publishers Weekly, Apr. 17, 2000, p.63
Time, May 8, 2000, p.97
USA Today, Apr. 19, 2000, p.D1

ADDRESS

Dutton Books/Penguin Putnam Inc.
375 Hudson Street
New York, NY 10014

E-mail: katie@katiet.com

WORLD WIDE WEB SITES

http://www.KatieT.com
http://www.safeteens.com
http://www.cyberangels.com
http://www.wiredkids.org
http://www.wiredteens.org
http://www.ftc.gov/bcp/conline/edcams/kidzprivacy/index.html

Photo and Illustration Credits

David Almond/Photos: Alex Telfer Photography; David Levenson/Black Star. Covers: HEAVEN EYES copyright © 2000 by David Almond. Jacket illustration by Cliff Nielsen. Jacket design by Alyssa Morris; KIT'S WILDERNESS copyright © 1999 by David Almond. Jacket illustration copyright © 2000 by Kamil Vojnar; SKELLIG copyright © 1998 by David Almond. Jacket illustration copyright © 1999 by Kamil Vojnar. All Random House Children's Books, a division of Random House, Inc.

Joan Bauer/Photo: Peter Serling. Covers: HOPE WAS HERE and SQUASHED courtesy G.P. Putnam's Sons and RULES OF THE ROAD courtesy Puffin Books, all Penguin Putnam Books for Young Readers; STICKS courtesy of Dell Yearling, an imprint of Random House Children's Books, a division of Random House, Inc.

Kate DiCamillo/Photo: Photo by Roberto Gonzalez/Orlando Sentinel. Covers: BECAUSE OF WINN-DIXIE copyright © 2000 by Kate DiCamillo; THE TIGER RISING copyright © 2001 by Kate DiCamillo.

Jack Gantos/Photo: Merry Scully. Covers: HEADS OR TAILS: STORIES FROM THE SIXTH GRADE copyright © 1994 by Jack Gantos. Jacket art copyright © 1994 by Beata Szpura; JACK ON THE TRACKS: FOUR SEASONS OF THE FIFTH GRADE copyright © 1999 by Jack Gantos. Jacket art copyright © 1999 by Beata Szpura; JOEY PIGZA LOSES CONTROL copyright © 2000 by Jack Gantos. Jacket art copyright © 2000 by Beata Szpura; JOEY PIGZA SWALLOWED THE KEY copyright © 1998 by Jack Gantos. Jacket art copyright © 1998 by Beata Szpura. All used with permission of Farrar, Straus and Giroux; BACK TO SCHOOL FOR ROTTEN RALPH courtesy of HarperCollins Publishers.

Aaron McGruder/Photo: BOONDOCKS cartoon and strip: BOONDOCKS copyright © Aaron McGruder. Dist. By UNIVERSAL PRESS SYNDICATE. Reprinted with permission. All rights reserved. Cover: FRESH FOR '01 . . . YOU SUCKAS! copyright © 2001 Aaron McGruder.

Richard Peck/Photo: Sonya Sones. Covers: ARE YOU IN THE HOUSE ALONE?; THE DREADFUL FUTURE OF BLOSSOM CULP; DREAMLAND LAKE and LOST IN CYBERSPACE all courtesy of Puffin Books, Penguin Putnam Books for Young Readers; FAIR WEATHER; A LONG WAY FROM CHICAGO and A YEAR DOWN YONDER all courtesy of Dial Books for Young Readers, a division of Penguin Putnam, Inc.; THE LAST SAFE PLACE ON EARTH courtesy of Dell Laurel-Leaf, an imprint of Random House Children's Books, a division of Random House, Inc.

Andrea Davis Pinkney/Photo: Dwight Carter. Covers: ALVIN AILEY text copyright © 1993 by Andrea Davis Pinkney. Illustrations copyright © 1993 by Brian Pinkney; DUKE ELLINGTON text copyright © 1998 by Andrea Davis Pinkney. Illustrations copyright © 1998 by Brian Pinkney; LET IT SHINE: STORIES OF BLACK WOMEN FREEDOM FIGHTERS text copyright © 2000 by Andrea Davis Pinkney. Illustrations copyright © 2000 by Stephen Alcorn; SILENT THUNDER: A CIVIL WAR STORY copyright © 1999 by Andrea Davis Pinkney; RAVEN IN A DOVE HOUSE courtesy Harcourt, Inc.

Louise Rennison/Photo: Scholastic LTD. Covers: ANGUS, THONGS AND FULL-FRONTAL SNOGGING and ON THE BRIGHT SIDE, I'M NOW THE GIRL-FRIEND OF A SEX GOD courtesy HarperCollins Publishers; KNOCKED OUT BY MY NUNGA-NUNGAS Picadilly Press UK edition.

David Small: Covers: EULALIE AND THE HOPPING HEAD copyright © 1982 by David Small. Illustration copyright © 1982 by David Small; THE GARDNER copyright © 1997 by Sarah Stewart. Illustration copyright © 1997 by David Small; THE JOURNEY copyright © 2001 by Sarah Stewart. Illustration copyright © 2001 by David Small, all used with permission of Farrar, Straus and Giroux; IMOGENE'S ANTLERS courtesy of Dragonfly Books, an imprint of Random House Children's Books, a division of Random House, Inc.; SO YOU WANT TO BE PRESIDENT? courtesy Philomel Books, Penguin Putnam Books for Young Readers.

Katie Tarbox/Photos: Alison E. Wachstein; AP/Wide World Photos; Kimberly Butler/TIMEPIX. Cover: KATIE.COM available from Plume Books, wherever fine books are sold.

How to Use the Cumulative Index

Our indexes have a new look. In an effort to make our indexes easier to use, we've combined the Name and General Index into a new, cumulative General Index. This single ready-reference resource covers all the volumes in *Biography Today,* both the general series and the special subject series. The new General Index contains complete listings of all individuals who have appeared in *Biography Today* since the series began. Their names appear in bold-faced type, followed by the issue in which they appear. The General Index also includes references for the occupations, nationalities, and ethnic and minority origins of individuals profiled in *Biography Today*.

We have also made some changes to our specialty indexes, the Places of Birth Index and the Birthday Index. To consolidate and to save space, the Places of Birth Index and the Birthday Index will no longer appear in the January and April issues of the softbound subscription series. But these indexes can still be found in the September issue of the softbound subscription series, in the hardbound Annual Cumulation at the end of each year, and in each volume of the special subject series.

General Series

The General Series of *Biography Today* is denoted in the index with the month and year of the issue in which the individual appeared. Each individual also appears in the Annual Cumulation for that year.

Bush, George W. . . . . Sep 00; Update 00; Update 01
Earnhardt, Dale . . . . Apr 01
Hill, Faith . . . . Sep 01
Holdsclaw, Chamique . . . . Sep 00
Kim Dae-jung . . . . Sep 01
L'Engle, Madeleine . . . . Jan 92; Apr 01
***N Sync** . . . . Jan 01
Payton, Walter . . . . Jan 00
Prinze, Freddie, Jr. . . . . Apr 00
Roberts, Julia . . . . Sep 01
Rowling, J.K. . . . . Sep 99; Update 00; Update 01
Spears, Britney . . . . Jan 01
Tucker, Chris . . . . Jan 01

Special Subject Series

The Special Subject Series of *Biography Today* are each denoted in the index with an abbreviated form of the series name, plus the number of the volume in which the individual appears. They are listed as follows.

Adams, Ansel . . . . Artist V.1 (Artists Series)
Bauer, Joan . . . . Author V.10 (Author Series)
Fanning, Shawn . . . . Science V.5 (Scientists & Inventors Series)
George, Eddie . . . . Sport V.6 (Sports Series)
Peterson, Roger Tory . . . . WorLdr V.1 (World Leaders Series: Environmental Leaders)
Sadat, Anwar . . . . WorLdr V.2 (World Leaders Series: Modern African Leaders)
Wolf, Hazel . . . . WorLdr V.3 (World Leaders Series: Environmental Leaders 2)

Updates

Updated information on selected individuals appears in the Appendix at the end of the *Biography Today* Annual Cumulation. In the index, the original entry is listed first, followed by any updates.

Arafat, Yasir . . . . Sep 94; Update 94; Update 95; Update 96; Update 97; Update 98; Update 00; Update 01
Gates, Bill . . . . Apr 93; Update 98; Update 00; Science V.5; Update 01
Griffith Joyner, Florence . . . . Sport V.1; Update 98
Sanders, Barry . . . . Sep 95; Update 99
Spock, Dr. Benjamin . . . . Sep 95; Update 98
Yeltsin, Boris . . . . Apr 92; Update 93; Update 95; Update 96; Update 98; Update 00

General Index

This index includes names, occupations, nationalities, and ethnic and minority origins that pertain to individuals profiled in *Biography Today*.

Places of Birth Index

The following index lists the places of birth for the individuals profiled in *Biography Today*. Places of birth are entered under state, province, and/or country.

Birthday Index

January		Year
1	Salinger, J.D.	1919
2	Asimov, Isaac	1920
4	Naylor, Phyllis Reynolds	1933
	Shula, Don	1930
7	Hurston, Zora Neale	?1891
	Rodriguez, Eloy	1947
8	Hawking, Stephen W.	1942
9	McLean, A.J.	1978
	Menchu, Rigoberta	1959
	Nixon, Richard	1913
11	Leopold, Aldo	1887
12	Amanpour, Christiane	1958
	Bezos, Jeff	1964
	Lasseter, John	?1957
	Limbaugh, Rush	1951
13	Webb, Alan	1983
14	Lucid, Shannon	1943
15	Werbach, Adam	1973
16	Fossey, Dian	1932
17	Carrey, Jim	1962
	Cormier, Robert	1925
	Jones, James Earl	1931
	Lewis, Shari	?1934
18	Ali, Muhammad	1942
	Messier, Mark	1961
19	Askins, Renee	1959
	Johnson, John	1918
21	Domingo, Placido	1941
	Nicklaus, Jack	1940
	Olajuwon, Hakeem	1963
22	Chavis, Benjamin	1948
	Ward, Lloyd D.	1949
23	Thiessen, Tiffani-Amber	1974
24	Haddock, Doris (Granny D)	1910
25	Alley, Kirstie	1955
26	Carter, Vince	1977
	Morita, Akio	1921
	Siskel, Gene	1946
	Tarbox, Katie	1982
27	Lester, Julius	1939
28	Carter, Nick	1980
	Fatone, Joey	1977
	Gretzky, Wayne	1961
29	Abbey, Edward	1927
	Gilbert, Sara	1975
	Hasek, Dominik	1965
	Peet, Bill	1915
	Winfrey, Oprah	1954
30	Alexander, Lloyd	1924
	Engelbart, Douglas	1925
31	Flannery, Sarah	1982
	Robinson, Jackie	1919
	Ryan, Nolan	1947
	Timberlake, Justin	1981

February		Year
1	Hughes, Langston	1902
	Spinelli, Jerry	1941
	Yeltsin, Boris	1931
3	Nixon, Joan Lowery	1927
	Rockwell, Norman	1894
4	Parks, Rosa	1913
5	Aaron, Hank	1934
6	Leakey, Mary	1913
	Rosa, Emily	1987
	Zmeskal, Kim	1976
7	Brooks, Garth	1962
	Wang, An	1920
	Wilder, Laura Ingalls	1867
8	Grisham, John	1955
9	Love, Susan	1948
10	Konigsburg, E.L.	1930
	Norman, Greg	1955
11	Aniston, Jennifer	1969
	Brandy	1979
	Rowland, Kelly	1981
	Yolen, Jane	1939
12	Blume, Judy	1938
	Kurzweil, Raymond	1948
	Small, David	1945
	Woodson, Jacqueline	?1964
13	Moss, Randy	1977
15	Groening, Matt	1954
	Jagr, Jaromir	1972
	Van Dyken, Amy	1973

December (continued)		Year
13	Fedorov, Sergei	1969
14	Jackson, Shirley	1916
15	Aidid, Mohammed Farah	1934
	Mendes, Chico	1944
16	Bailey, Donovan	1967
	McCary, Michael	1971
	Mead, Margaret	1901
17	Kielburger, Craig	1982
18	Aguilera, Christina	1980
	Holmes, Katie	1978
	Pitt, Brad	1964
	Sanchez Vicario, Arantxa	1971
	Spielberg, Steven	1947
19	Morrison, Sam	1936
	Sapp, Warren	1972
	White, Reggie	1961
20	Uchida, Mitsuko	1948
	Zirkle, Aliy	1969
21	Evert, Chris	1954
	Griffith Joyner, Florence	1959
	Stiles, Jackie	1978
	Webb, Karrie	1974
22	Pinkney, Jerry	1939
23	Avi	1937
	Harbaugh, Jim	1963
	Lowman, Meg	1953
24	Lowe, Alex	1958
	Martin, Ricky	1971
25	Sadat, Anwar	1918
26	Butcher, Susan	1954
27	Roberts, Cokie	1943
28	Lee, Stan	1922
	Washington, Denzel	1954
30	Woods, Tiger	1975

Biography Today
General Series

"*Biography Today* will be useful in elementary and middle school libraries and in public library children's collections where there is a need for biographies of current personalities. High schools serving reluctant readers may also want to consider a subscription."

— *Booklist,* American Library Association

"Highly recommended for the young adult audience. Readers will delight in the accessible, energetic, tell-all style; teachers, librarians, and parents will welcome the clever format, intelligent and informative text. It should prove especially useful in motivating "reluctant" readers or literate nonreaders."

— *MultiCultural Review*

"Written in a friendly, almost chatty tone, the profiles offer quick, objective information. While coverage of current figures makes *Biography Today* a useful reference tool, an appealing format and wide scope make it a fun resource to browse." — *School Library Journal*

"The best source for current information at a level kids can understand."

— Kelly Bryant, School Librarian, Carlton, OR

"Easy for kids to read. We love it! Don't want to be without it."

— Lynn McWhirter, School Librarian, Rockford, IL

Biography Today **General Series** includes a unique combination of current biographical profiles that teachers and librarians — and the readers themselves — tell us are most appealing. The **General Series** is available as a 3-issue subscription; hardcover annual cumulation; or subscription plus cumulation.

Within the **General Series**, your readers will find a variety of sketches about:

- Authors
- Musicians
- Political leaders
- Sports figures
- Movie actresses & actors
- Cartoonists
- Scientists
- Astronauts
- TV personalities
- and the movers & shakers in many other fields!

ONE-YEAR SUBSCRIPTION

- 3 softcover issues, 6" x 9"
- Published in January, April, and September
- 1-year subscription, $57
- 150 pages per issue
- 10-12 profiles per issue
- Contact sources for additional information
- Cumulative General, Places of Birth, and Birthday Indexes

HARDBOUND ANNUAL CUMULATION

- Sturdy 6" x 9" hardbound volume
- Published in December
- $58 per volume
- 450 pages per volume
- 30-36 profiles — includes all profiles found in softcover issues for that calendar year
- Cumulative General, Places of Birth, and Birthday Indexes
- Special appendix features current updates of previous profiles

SUBSCRIPTION AND CUMULATION COMBINATION

- $99 for 3 softcover issues plus the hardbound volume

1992

Paula Abdul
Andre Agassi
Kirstie Alley
Terry Anderson
Roseanne Arnold
Isaac Asimov
James Baker
Charles Barkley
Larry Bird
Judy Blume
Berke Breathed
Garth Brooks
Barbara Bush
George Bush
Fidel Castro
Bill Clinton
Bill Cosby
Diana, Princess of Wales
Shannen Doherty
Elizabeth Dole
David Duke
Gloria Estefan
Mikhail Gorbachev
Steffi Graf
Wayne Gretzky
Matt Groening
Alex Haley
Hammer
Martin Handford
Stephen Hawking
Hulk Hogan
Saddam Hussein
Lee Iacocca
Bo Jackson
Mae Jemison
Peter Jennings
Steven Jobs
Pope John Paul II
Magic Johnson
Michael Jordon
Jackie Joyner-Kersee
Spike Lee
Mario Lemieux
Madeleine L'Engle
Jay Leno
Yo-Yo Ma
Nelson Mandela
Wynton Marsalis
Thurgood Marshall
Ann Martin
Barbara McClintock
Emily Arnold McCully
Antonia Novello
Sandra Day O'Connor
Rosa Parks
Jane Pauley
H. Ross Perot
Luke Perry
Scottie Pippen
Colin Powell
Jason Priestley
Queen Latifah
Yitzhak Rabin
Sally Ride
Pete Rose
Nolan Ryan
H. Norman Schwarzkopf
Jerry Seinfeld
Dr. Seuss
Gloria Steinem
Clarence Thomas
Chris Van Allsburg
Cynthia Voigt
Bill Watterson
Robin Williams
Oprah Winfrey
Kristi Yamaguchi
Boris Yeltsin

1993

Maya Angelou
Arthur Ashe
Avi
Kathleen Battle
Candice Bergen
Boutros Boutros-Ghali
Chris Burke
Dana Carvey
Cesar Chavez
Henry Cisneros
Hillary Rodham Clinton
Jacques Cousteau
Cindy Crawford
Macaulay Culkin
Lois Duncan
Marian Wright Edelman
Cecil Fielder
Bill Gates
Sara Gilbert
Dizzy Gillespie
Al Gore
Cathy Guisewite
Jasmine Guy
Anita Hill
Ice-T
Darci Kistler
k.d. lang
Dan Marino
Rigoberta Menchu
Walter Dean Myers
Martina Navratilova
Phyllis Reynolds Naylor
Rudolf Nureyev
Shaquille O'Neal
Janet Reno
Jerry Rice
Mary Robinson
Winona Ryder
Jerry Spinelli
Denzel Washington
Keenen Ivory Wayans
Dave Winfield

1994

Tim Allen
Marian Anderson
Mario Andretti
Ned Andrews
Yasir Arafat
Bruce Babbitt
Mayim Bialik
Bonnie Blair
Ed Bradley
John Candy
Mary Chapin Carpenter
Benjamin Chavis
Connie Chung
Beverly Cleary
Kurt Cobain
F.W. de Klerk
Rita Dove
Linda Ellerbee
Sergei Fedorov
Zlata Filipovic
Daisy Fuentes
Ruth Bader Ginsburg
Whoopi Goldberg
Tonya Harding
Melissa Joan Hart
Geoff Hooper
Whitney Houston
Dan Jansen
Nancy Kerrigan
Alexi Lalas
Charlotte Lopez
Wilma Mankiller
Shannon Miller
Toni Morrison
Richard Nixon
Greg Norman
Severo Ochoa
River Phoenix
Elizabeth Pine
Jonas Salk
Richard Scarry
Emmitt Smith
Will Smith
Steven Spielberg
Patrick Stewart
R.L. Stine
Lewis Thomas
Barbara Walters
Charlie Ward
Steve Young
Kim Zmeskal

1995

Troy Aikman
Jean-Bertrand Aristide
Oksana Baiul
Halle Berry
Benazir Bhutto
Jonathan Brandis
Warren E. Burger
Ken Burns
Candace Cameron
Jimmy Carter
Agnes de Mille
Placido Domingo
Janet Evans
Patrick Ewing
Newt Gingrich
John Goodman
Amy Grant
Jesse Jackson
James Earl Jones
Julie Krone
David Letterman
Rush Limbaugh
Heather Locklear
Reba McEntire
Joe Montana
Cosmas Ndeti
Hakeem Olajuwon
Ashley Olsen
Mary-Kate Olsen
Jennifer Parkinson
Linus Pauling
Itzhak Perlman
Cokie Roberts
Wilma Rudolph
Salt 'N' Pepa
Barry Sanders
William Shatner
Elizabeth George Speare
Dr. Benjamin Spock
Jonathan Taylor Thomas
Vicki Van Meter
Heather Whitestone
Pedro Zamora

1996

Aung San Suu Kyi
Boyz II Men
Brandy
Ron Brown
Mariah Carey
Jim Carrey
Larry Champagne III
Christo
Chelsea Clinton
Coolio
Bob Dole
David Duchovny
Debbi Fields
Chris Galeczka
Jerry Garcia
Jennie Garth
Wendy Guey
Tom Hanks
Alison Hargreaves
Sir Edmund Hillary
Judith Jamison
Barbara Jordan
Annie Leibovitz
Carl Lewis
Jim Lovell
Mickey Mantle
Lynn Margulis
Iqbal Masih
Mark Messier
Larisa Oleynik
Christopher Pike
David Robinson
Dennis Rodman
Selena
Monica Seles
Don Shula
Kerri Strug
Tiffani-Amber Thiessen
Dave Thomas
Jaleel White

1997

Madeleine Albright
Marcus Allen
Gillian Anderson
Rachel Blanchard
Zachery Ty Bryan
Adam Ezra Cohen
Claire Danes
Celine Dion
Jean Driscoll
Louis Farrakhan
Ella Fitzgerald
Harrison Ford
Bryant Gumbel
John Johnson
Michael Johnson
Maya Lin
George Lucas
John Madden
Bill Monroe
Alanis Morissette
Sam Morrison
Rosie O'Donnell
Muammar el-Qaddafi
Christopher Reeve
Pete Sampras
Pat Schroeder
Rebecca Sealfon
Tupac Shakur
Tabitha Soren
Herbert Tarvin
Merlin Tuttle
Mara Wilson

1998

Bella Abzug
Kofi Annan
Neve Campbell
Sean Combs (Puff Daddy)
Dalai Lama (Tenzin Gyatso)
Diana, Princess of Wales
Leonardo DiCaprio
Walter E. Diemer
Ruth Handler
Hanson
Livan Hernandez
Jewel
Jimmy Johnson
Tara Lipinski
Jody-Anne Maxwell
Dominique Moceanu
Alexandra Nechita
Brad Pitt
LeAnn Rimes
Emily Rosa
David Satcher
Betty Shabazz
Kordell Stewart
Shinichi Suzuki
Mother Teresa
Mike Vernon
Reggie White
Kate Winslet

1999

Ben Affleck
Jennifer Aniston
Maurice Ashley
Kobe Bryant
Bessie Delany
Sadie Delany
Sharon Draper
Sarah Michelle Gellar
John Glenn
Savion Glover
Jeff Gordon
David Hampton
Lauryn Hill
King Hussein
Lynn Johnston
Shari Lewis
Oseola McCarty
Mark McGwire
Slobodan Milosevic
Natalie Portman
J. K. Rowling
Frank Sinatra
Gene Siskel
Sammy Sosa
John Stanford
Natalia Toro
Shania Twain
Mitsuko Uchida
Jesse Ventura
Venus Williams

2000

Christina Aguilera
K.A. Applegate
Lance Armstrong
Backstreet Boys
Daisy Bates
Harry Blackmun
George W. Bush
Carson Daly
Ron Dayne
Henry Louis Gates, Jr.
Doris Haddock (Granny D)
Jennifer Love Hewitt
Chamique Holdsclaw
Katie Holmes
Charlayne Hunter-Gault
Johanna Johnson
Craig Kielburger
John Lasseter
Peyton Manning
Ricky Martin
John McCain
Walter Payton
Freddie Prinze, Jr.
Viviana Risca
Briana Scurry
George Thampy
CeCe Winans

2001

Jessica Alba
Christiane Amanpour
Drew Barrymore
Jeff Bezos
Destiny's Child
Dale Earnhardt
Carly Fiorina
Aretha Franklin
Cathy Freeman
Tony Hawk
Faith Hill
Kim Dae-jung
Madeleine L'Engle
Mariangela Lisanti
Frankie Muniz
*N Sync
Ellen Ochoa
Jeff Probst
Julia Roberts
Carl T. Rowan
Britney Spears
Chris Tucker
Lloyd D. Ward
Alan Webb
Chris Weinke

Biography Today

Subject Series

Expands and complements the General Series and targets specific subject areas . . .

Our readers asked for it! They wanted more biographies, and the *Biography Today* **Subject Series** is our response to that demand. Now your readers can choose their special areas of interest and go on to read about their favorites in those fields. Priced at just $39 per volume, the following specific volumes are included in the *Biography Today* **Subject Series**:

- **Artists Series**
- **Author Series**
- **Scientists & Inventors Series**
- **Sports Series**
- **World Leaders Series**
  Environmental Leaders
  Modern African Leaders

FEATURES AND FORMAT

- Sturdy 6" x 9" hardbound volumes
- Individual volumes, $39 each
- 200 pages per volume
- 10-12 profiles per volume — targets individuals within a specific subject area
- Contact sources for additional information
- Cumulative General, Places of Birth, and Birthday Indexes

NOTE: There is ***no duplication of entries*** between the **General Series** of *Biography Today* and the **Subject Series.**

AUTHOR SERIES

"A useful tool for children's assignment needs." — *School Library Journal*

"The prose is workmanlike: report writers will find enough detail to begin sound investigations, and browsers are likely to find someone of interest." — *School Library Journal*

SCIENTISTS & INVENTORS SERIES

"The articles are readable, attractively laid out, and touch on important points that will suit assignment needs. Browsers will note the clear writing and interesting details." — *School Library Journal*

"The book is excellent for demonstrating that scientists are real people with widely diverse backgrounds and personal interests. The biographies are fascinating to read." — *The Science Teacher*

SPORTS SERIES

"This series should become a standard resource in libraries that serve intermediate students." — *School Library Journal*

ENVIRONMENTAL LEADERS #1

"A tremendous book that fills a gap in the biographical category of books. This is a great reference book." — *Science Scope*

Artists Series

VOLUME 1

Ansel Adams
Romare Bearden
Margaret Bourke-White
Alexander Calder
Marc Chagall
Helen Frankenthaler
Jasper Johns
Jacob Lawrence
Henry Moore
Grandma Moses
Louise Nevelson
Georgia O'Keeffe
Gordon Parks
I.M. Pei
Diego Rivera
Norman Rockwell
Andy Warhol
Frank Lloyd Wright

Author Series

VOLUME 1

Eric Carle
Alice Childress
Robert Cormier
Roald Dahl
Jim Davis
John Grisham
Virginia Hamilton
James Herriot
S.E. Hinton
M.E. Kerr
Stephen King
Gary Larson
Joan Lowery Nixon
Gary Paulsen
Cynthia Rylant
Mildred D. Taylor
Kurt Vonnegut, Jr.
E.B. White
Paul Zindel

VOLUME 2

James Baldwin
Stan and Jan Berenstain
David Macaulay
Patricia MacLachlan
Scott O'Dell
Jerry Pinkney
Jack Prelutsky
Lynn Reid Banks
Faith Ringgold
J.D. Salinger
Charles Schulz
Maurice Sendak
P.L. Travers
Garth Williams

VOLUME 3

Candy Dawson Boyd
Ray Bradbury
Gwendolyn Brooks
Ralph W. Ellison
Louise Fitzhugh
Jean Craighead George
E.L. Konigsburg
C.S. Lewis
Fredrick L. McKissack
Patricia C. McKissack
Katherine Paterson
Anne Rice
Shel Silverstein
Laura Ingalls Wilder

VOLUME 4

Betsy Byars
Chris Carter
Caroline B. Cooney
Christopher Paul Curtis
Anne Frank
Robert Heinlein
Marguerite Henry
Lois Lowry
Melissa Mathison
Bill Peet
August Wilson

VOLUME 5

Sharon Creech
Michael Crichton
Karen Cushman
Tomie dePaola
Lorraine Hansberry
Karen Hesse
Brian Jacques
Gary Soto
Richard Wright
Laurence Yep

VOLUME 6

Lloyd Alexander
Paula Danziger
Nancy Farmer
Zora Neale Hurston
Shirley Jackson
Angela Johnson
Jon Krakauer
Leo Lionni
Francine Pascal
Louis Sachar
Kevin Williamson

VOLUME 7

William H. Armstrong
Patricia Reilly Giff
Langston Hughes
Stan Lee
Julius Lester
Robert Pinsky
Todd Strasser
Jacqueline Woodson
Patricia C. Wrede
Jane Yolen

VOLUME 8

Amelia Atwater-Rhodes
Barbara Cooney
Paul Laurence Dunbar
Ursula K. Le Guin
Farley Mowat
Naomi Shihab Nye
Daniel Pinkwater
Beatrix Potter
Ann Rinaldi

VOLUME 9

Robb Armstrong
Cherie Bennett
Bruce Coville
Rosa Guy
Harper Lee
Irene Gut Opdyke
Philip Pullman
Jon Scieszka
Amy Tan
Joss Whedon

VOLUME 10

David Almond
Joan Bauer
Kate DiCamillo
Jack Gantos
Aaron McGruder
Richard Peck
Andrea Davis Pinkney
Louise Rennison
David Small
Katie Tarbox

Scientists & Inventors Series

VOLUME 1

John Bardeen
Sylvia Earle
Dian Fossey
Jane Goodall
Bernadine Healy
Jack Horner
Mathilde Krim
Edwin Land
Louise & Mary Leakey
Rita Levi-Montalcini
J. Robert Oppenheimer
Albert Sabin
Carl Sagan
James D. Watson

VOLUME 2

Jane Brody
Seymour Cray
Paul Erdös
Walter Gilbert
Stephen Jay Gould
Shirley Ann Jackson
Raymond Kurzweil
Shannon Lucid
Margaret Mead
Garrett Morgan
Bill Nye
Eloy Rodriguez
An Wang

VOLUME 3

Luis W. Alvarez
Hans A. Bethe
Gro Harlem Brundtland
Mary S. Calderone
Ioana Dumitriu
Temple Grandin
John Langston Gwaltney
Bernard Harris
Jerome Lemelson
Susan Love
Ruth Patrick
Oliver Sacks
Richie Stachowski

VOLUME 4

David Attenborough
Robert Ballard
Ben Carson
Eileen Collins
Biruté Galdikas
Lonnie Johnson
Meg Lowman
Forrest Mars Sr.
Akio Morita
Janese Swanson

VOLUME 5

Steve Case
Douglas Engelbart
Shawn Fanning
Sarah Flannery
Bill Gates
Laura Groppe
Grace Murray Hopper
Steven Jobs
Rand and Robyn Miller
Shigeru Miyamoto
Steve Wozniak

Sports Series

VOLUME 1

Hank Aaron
Kareem Abdul-Jabbar
Hassiba Boulmerka
Susan Butcher
Beth Daniel
Chris Evert
Ken Griffey, Jr.
Florence Griffith Joyner
Grant Hill
Greg LeMond
Pelé
Uta Pippig
Cal Ripken, Jr.
Arantxa Sanchez Vicario
Deion Sanders
Tiger Woods

VOLUME 2

Muhammad Ali
Donovan Bailey
Gail Devers
John Elway
Brett Favre
Mia Hamm
Anfernee "Penny" Hardaway
Martina Hingis
Gordie Howe
Jack Nicklaus
Richard Petty
Dot Richardson
Sheryl Swoopes
Steve Yzerman

VOLUME 3

Joe Dumars
Jim Harbaugh
Dominik Hasek
Michelle Kwan
Rebecca Lobo
Greg Maddux
Fatuma Roba
Jackie Robinson
John Stockton
Picabo Street
Pat Summitt
Amy Van Dyken

VOLUME 4

Wilt Chamberlain
Brandi Chastain
Derek Jeter
Karch Kiraly
Alex Lowe
Randy Moss
Se Ri Pak
Dawn Riley
Karen Smyers
Kurt Warner
Serena Williams

VOLUME 5

Vince Carter
Lindsay Davenport
Lisa Fernandez
Fu Mingxia
Jaromir Jagr
Marion Jones
Pedro Martinez
Warren Sapp
Jenny Thompson
Karrie Webb

VOLUME 6

Jennifer Capriati
Stacy Dragila
Kevin Garnett
Eddie George
Alex Rodriguez
Joe Sakic
Annika Sorenstam
Jackie Stiles
Tiger Woods
Aliy Zirkle

World Leaders Series

VOLUME 1: Environmental Leaders 1

Edward Abbey
Renee Askins
David Brower
Rachel Carson
Marjory Stoneman Douglas
Dave Foreman
Lois Gibbs
Wangari Maathai
Chico Mendes
Russell A. Mittermeier
Margaret and Olaus J. Murie
Patsy Ruth Oliver
Roger Tory Peterson
Ken Saro-Wiwa
Paul Watson
Adam Werbach

VOLUME 2: Modern African Leaders

Mohammed Farah Aidid
Idi Amin
Hastings Kamuzu Banda
Haile Selassie
Hassan II
Kenneth Kaunda
Jomo Kenyatta
Winnie Mandela
Mobutu Sese Seko
Robert Mugabe
Kwame Nkrumah
Julius Kambarage Nyerere
Anwar Sadat
Jonas Savimbi
Léopold Sédar Senghor
William V. S. Tubman

VOLUME 3: Environmental Leaders 2

John Cronin
Dai Qing
Ka Hsaw Wa
Winona LaDuke
Aldo Leopold
Bernard Martin
Cynthia Moss
John Muir
Gaylord Nelson
Douglas Tompkins
Hazel Wolf